SCANDALIZE MY NAME

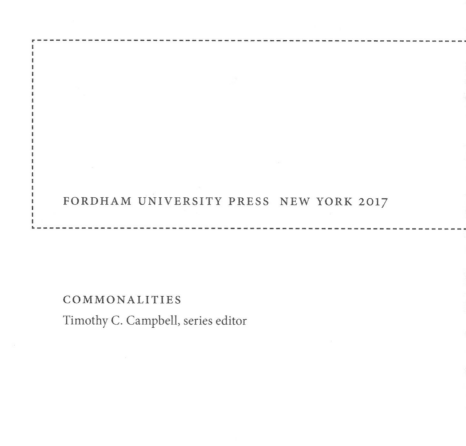

FORDHAM UNIVERSITY PRESS NEW YORK 2017

COMMONALITIES
Timothy C. Campbell, series editor

SCANDALIZE MY NAME

Black Feminist Practice and the Making

of Black Social Life

TERRION L. WILLIAMSON

Visit us online at www.fordhampress.com.

Library of Congress Cataloging-in-Publication Data available online at catalog.loc.gov.

Printed in the United States of America

19 18 17   5 4 3 2 1

First edition

THE
AMERICAN
LITERATURES
INITIATIVE

A book in the American Literatures Initiative (ALI), a collaborative publishing project of NYU Press, Fordham University Press, Rutgers University Press, Temple University Press, and the University of Virginia Press. The Initiative is supported by The Andrew W. Mellon Foundation. For more information, please visit www.americanliteratures.org.

For Grammy

CONTENTS

INTRODUCTION

Back to Living Again

When we are not "public," with all that the word connotes for black people then how do we live and who are we?

—ELIZABETH ALEXANDER, *THE BLACK INTERIOR*

The notion that black culture is some kind of backwater or tributary of an American "mainstream" is well established in much popular as well as standard social science literature. To the prudent black American masses, however, core black culture *is* the mainstream.

—JOHN LANGSTON GWALTNEY, *DRYLONGSO*

First, a story.

I was twenty-one years old, a senior at the University of Illinois at Chicago, when, after three years of immersion into what passed as "the college experience" on that campus, I achieved the ultimate in adult-lite independence: I moved into my own apartment. It was the top unit of an old but well-maintained three-unit building on Eighty-First Street nestled between Ashland and Damen in the Auburn Gresham neighborhood, which, as you might know, is the South Side of Chicago. And what you might also know, or at least suspect, is that this was not the South Side of the Obamas. We're not talking about Hyde Park here. I was living on the South Side of the "people" whose reputation for violence has made any number of national headlines but where, despite said reputation, all manner of black folk freely roam, the residents routinely put trash cans and fold-out chairs in their parking spots to keep them from being taken, the streets and sidewalks transform into playgrounds and waterparks on sticky summer days, and there are as many storefront churches as there are liquor stores and chicken joints.

Though I do not come from the great state of Chicago, I do come from one of its suburbs. Actually, that's not true. My hometown is not a suburb of Chicago and neither is Chicago a state, of course, but when you come from Peoria, a city with a total population of about 116,000 and a black population of approximately 30,000, you learn to think of it as such. You learn that the best way to explain to non-Illinoisans, as well as many Chicagoans, where Peoria is located is in reference to Chicago (Peoria is approximately 170 miles southwest) and that its significance is typically best understood in relationship to two of its most noteworthy successes: Caterpillar, the Fortune 500 heavy-machinery manufacturer that is headquartered there and has historically employed a significant number of its residents, and the late great social commentator Richard Pryor, who was born there in 1940 (and not necessarily in that order). Anyway, the point is, the South Side of Peoria, with its masses of black people cordoned off into the most underresourced area of the city, the place where I was born and raised, is not unlike the South Side of Chicago, which became the location of my first real foray into adulthood.

For five hundred dollars a month plus utilities I had a space that was all mine, where I could come and go as I pleased, where I didn't have to check my guests in and out, where I didn't have a curfew, where I didn't have to pick up and search out a place to sleep when my roommate had "company," where I could decorate without getting anyone else's input, where I could be as clean or as messy as I wanted (though, as it turned out, I was much less inclined toward messiness when I was the one paying the bills). I was ecstatic. My parents, I later found out, were not. They were slightly terrified—particularly my dad, a self-proclaimed "country boy" who is currently a resident of the blink-and-you'll-miss-it Delta town of Gunnison, Mississippi (population: 452), who never did approve of "that big ole raggedy city" anyway. But, alas, that little third-floor, one-bedroom apartment, complete with its secondhand furniture and rodent interlopers, was where I established my first self-made home.

Despite whatever fears my dads—my biological father and my stepfather—might have had about their young, single, relatively sheltered daughter living alone on the South Side of Chicago, they did what they have always done and rallied together with my mothers—my biological mother and stepmother—and grandmothers to support me in my big-girl endeavors. But I remember it being my Grammy, my mother's mother, who, though she was never to see my apartment in person herself, seemed most excited for me. Soon after moving into my place I received a care package from her containing household provisions, including a recipe book made up of her own handed-down recipes and a document she'd typed up outlining remedies for various minor catastrophes like ink-stained clothing and stubborn grease stains. Not long after that I went to visit her, and as we were sitting in her kitchen catching up on things and talking about my adventures in homemaking, I told her about how I was rather liking "keeping house." And I still remember very clearly her turning to me and saying, "See, it's not so bad taking care of your home and family, is it?"

It was such a simple, unassuming, and, ultimately, rhetorical question, but for reasons I did not at all understand at the time, that moment stayed with me. It was not until after she died in August 2007, while I was a graduate student in the thick of studying for my PhD comprehensive exams, that I began to fully appreciate what Grammy had been saying to me all those years before. Because it was not until then that I really began to contemplate the meaning of my grandmother's life and its impact not just on my life but also on the shaping of my life's work.

My grandmother, whose full name was Bernice Lee Turner (née Collier), was born in 1931, the fourth of five children, and lived most of her life in Danville, Illinois, a city about 150 miles southeast of Peoria that is so small Peoria is a "big ole raggedy city" in comparison. She had three children, a son named Jacque and my mother, Kim, who were born to her first husband, whom she divorced in 1960, and another son, Brett, who was born to her second husband, who died unexpectedly of health complications in 1970. She married for the final time in 1987. She worked at several different companies throughout her life, including the Internal Revenue Service in Detroit, where she lived for several years with her first husband before returning to Danville, and the Danville Housing Authority. Her longest continuous period of employment was at the First Midwest Bank in Danville, where she held various positions, including manager of teller operations, before retiring in 1993 after more than twenty-five years of service.

Despite a seemingly rewarding career, the center of my grandmother's joy was her family, and there was nothing she loved as much as gathering with her children, grandchildren, siblings, nieces, nephews, and whoever else might happen to stop through, around a meal she had labored over for hours (years after my parents divorced, my father would still go into a near drool when talking about my Grammy's macaroni and cheese, arguably the most famous of her famous dishes). And because I was her oldest and, for a number of years, only biological grandchild and her only daughter's only daughter, I had an especially close relationship with her. Growing up, I spent countless hours standing by her side and, occasionally, helping as she cooked in her kitchen; laying in her living-room floor cutting paper dolls out of the *Jet* and *Ebony* magazines she would save for me; sitting underneath her arm at Union Missionary Baptist Church while the organist, my uncle, played what was to me at that time absolutely *terrifying* "shouting" music; watching movies with her that I'd convinced her to rent because they were R-rated and my mother never would; making sugary-sweet coffee under her watch (because, like R-rated movies, coffee was something my mother did not allow her adolescent daughter); and going on summer vacations with her and my grandfather and younger cousin to places like St. Louis and the Wisconsin Dells. And we would talk and talk. There was very little that was off-limits between my grandmother and me. I never felt from her the judgment that I felt in other places and with other people, and it was with her alone that I was my most vulnerable, most joyful, most complete self.

But for all our talking and all our sharing, there are particular things I do not remember about my grandmother. I do not, for instance, remember her talking much about money, at least, not about how to get more of it—although she never, at any point in her life, had a whole lot more than just enough to get by. Nor do I remember her ever spending a lot of time trying to figure out how to amass material things. Now, please believe, Aunt Becie (as my cousins called her) was quite the fashion plate, and she enjoyed the finer things in life when she could. But the material things she enjoyed were by-products of a life well lived and not, in and of themselves, her reason for living. Moreover, even before her retirement she never prioritized material or immaterial "stuff" so much that she did not have time to cook for her family or spend time in her garden or sing in the church choir or visit with her friends or tend to her children. Which is to say, her life was full of doing the things she loved to do.

And when it came to me, her beloved granddaughter, I never remember my grandmother telling me that I needed to go out and make a "success" of myself. Her stated goals for me never did include attending prestigious schools or earning a lot of money or having elite degrees or fancy titles or having a high-profile job. This is not to say that she was not extremely proud of me when I did do some of those things. I remember, for instance, near the end of her life when I was in law school and had published my first journal article. I had given my mother a reprint of the article to give to my grandmother when she went to visit her at the nursing home she was living in by then, and afterward my mother called me, laughter in her voice. She told me that when Grammy saw it she had broken into tears, saying she didn't really know what in the world I was talking about but she was just happy because I was "so smart." But the thing is this: Grammy did indeed know what I was talking about. Perhaps she did not understand all of the intricacies of tribal sovereignty and the like that I was attempting to work through in that elusive document that is the law review note (and, to be quite honest, neither did I), but she did understand the struggle for self-governance, the need to carve out a space of one's own, to claim it and to hold onto it and to demand it. And in the relay between my Grammy's tears and my Mama's laugh was, and is, a whole realm of comprehension that I am only now able to lay even a modicum of claim to.

Though my grandmother was most certainly one of my biggest cheerleaders and supporters while she was living, what she wanted most for me was bound up in that long-ago statement she made to me affirming the value of homemaking. The point is not to be taken literally; she was not saying that I necessarily had to become a wife and mother as she did. Instead, what I eventually heard my grandmother telling me, via both our conversations and the example of her life, was that tending to her home, cooking, cleaning, and the like, were not burdens from which she hoped to escape but acts of love that helped to sustain her as much as they did her family. Further, she was telling me that her life was not circumscribed by the conditions of its possibility but was instead enriched and enlarged by her embrace of the mundane and the everyday. I believe that more than outward signifiers of success, what my grandmother ultimately wanted for me and all of her children and grandchildren was that we realize, in accordance with Ralph Ellison and a whole host of other black folks who came before and after her, "the attitudes and values which give Negro American life its sense of wholeness and which render it bearable and human and, when measured by our own terms, *desirable*."[1]

This desire of my grandmother's resonates with the experience Rita Dove relates of making a dress for her daughter during a sabbatical she took not long after winning the Pulitzer Prize in Poetry in 1987. Despite the protests of her husband, who thought she was wasting her precious sabbatical time by making her daughter a lace "princess dress" for her fifth birthday that she was sure to destroy before her party's end, Dove spent the time necessary to make it so that her daughter would "ha[ve] the dress she wanted," referring to the making of it as "fieldwork" for a poem she was working on.[2] Though my grandmother was neither a poet nor a scholar in the traditional sense, her cooking functioned similarly to Dove's dressmaking. She would spend hours shopping, prepping, cleaning, picking, cutting, dicing, chopping, baking, and frying in preparation for a meal that would often be devoured without much fanfare in a matter of minutes. But I imagine Grammy might have also thought about this as fieldwork, perhaps not for a poem, but for the making of a life worth living.

Telling this story of my grandmother is meant neither to glamorize her life nor to suggest that her life was wholly unique (though she was, of course, uniquely special to me). Indeed, as a black woman who came of age in the segregated North of the 1930s and 1940s, who did not have much in the way of a formal education beyond high school, who divorced one husband, buried another, and had a tumultuous relationship with the third, who experienced a seventeen-year stretch during which she was, in her words, "looking for love," who was episodically a single mother of multiple children, and who was ravaged for years by Parkinson's disease before her eventual death, there was much that was difficult and painful in her life.[3] And it is, by most accounts, a story black women know well.

Yet the story of my grandmother is important to this project for a couple of reasons. For one, it helps to reveal the contours of a black feminist practice that need not be tethered to discussions of movements, organizations, or overt political activism. To my knowledge, my grandmother was never actively involved in any national or local social justice or political organizations—her organizational commitments were mostly limited to church groups like the choir and usher board—and I doubt that at any point in her life she would have identified herself as a feminist. The same is probably also true of my mother. But my mother and grandmother have both been instrumental in my own coming to feminism. Because although they may not be or have been feminists in the academic sense of the term, and despite certain ideological differences we may have or have had, they have taught me more about what it means to resist oppression, demand accountability, struggle for voice, and cherish all people than anyone or anything else.

I am not treading any particularly new ground here, for black feminist thinkers within the academy have often been concerned with grounding their work in the experiences of women working outside the academy, particularly those from poor and working-class backgrounds. In *Black Feminist Thought*, one of the seminal texts in the black feminist "canon," Patricia Hill Collins discusses the tremendous influence black women who are not academics have had on the evolution of black feminist thought:

> Developing Black feminist thought as critical social theory involves including the ideas of Black women not previously considered intellectuals—many of whom may be working-class women with jobs outside academia—as well as those emanating from more formal, legitimated scholarship. The ideas we share with one another as mothers in extended families, as othermothers in Black communities, as members of Black churches, and as teachers to the Black community's children have formed one pivotal area where African-American women have hammered out multifaceted Black women's standpoint.[4]

For Hill Collins black feminist practice is a distinct outgrowth of black feminist thought, which is to say it is an outcome of black feminism.[5] Here I make a different sort of distinction. While I do not draw a dividing line between thought and practice, I do distinguish between black feminist practice and black feminism, which, in alignment with the Combahee River Collective and other black feminist thinkers, I define as a sustained sociopolitical commitment to centering the lives of black women and girls while actively struggling against racism, sexism, heterosexism, classism, and other intersecting modalities of oppression that affect even those who do not identify as either black or female.[6] I define black feminist practice as a radical commitment to the significance of black female life and the humanity of all black peoples, regardless of whether the practitioner identifies with feminism as a formalized ideological commitment or holds some views that might ultimately be deemed antithetical to feminism itself. Under these terms, thought is not a separate endeavor but a constituent element of the critical engagement. Thus what it means to take up "practice" here is to turn our attention to "the politics of the everyday,"[7] the places "where the subject lives as theorist, consumer, grocery shopper, got-to-pick-up-the-mail-now, let's go to the bank."[8]

My grandmother's story is also important because it works to turn the aspirational posturing that often characterizes black racial uplift narratives on its head. By way of example, in an interview actor Kerry Washington gave to Oprah Winfrey in late 2012, she discussed the intersection of two of her most high-profile roles—Olivia Pope, the powerful D.C. fixer and one-time presidential mistress who headlines *Scandal*, the hit television series produced for ABC by Shonda Rhimes, and Broomhilda Von Shaft, the slave wife in Quentin Tarantino's 2012 film *Django Unchained*. In the interview Washington stated that Olivia Pope is "the answer to Broomhilda's prayers about what might be possible someday" and that Olivia Pope and Broomhilda Von Shaft are "the same woman hundreds of years apart." To which Winfrey responded, "That is so perfect I could weep."[9]

Washington's proclamation on its face might be innocent enough and, aside from Pope's stint as a mistress, one that perhaps many black women would agree with. To be sure, Olivia Pope lives a life that is hard to imagine for many black women today, let alone a slave woman living in the mid-nineteenth century. But this is actually the heart of the thing. Because for the vast majority of black women living today, becoming an Olivia Pope is about as likely a possibility as it would have been for Broomhilda Von Shaft in 1858, and the reasons for this have little if anything to do with ability or work ethic. And so one wonders about the ascription of those values and traits that would be required for a black woman to become Olivia Pope, an expensively dressed, prototypically beautiful, incidentally black, upper-class Washington insider who is bedding the presumptive leader of the free world, to the slave woman.[10]

It is a quandary that actually does matter, not because there is necessarily anything wrong with wanting to be wealthy or powerful or successful (although we might contemplate just what it means to attain these things in the face of modern-day capitalism and its organizing principles) but because the line of descent Washington and Winfrey mark out for black women ignores a whole range of black female possibility. It would be one thing if this moment could be simply dismissed as the inconsequential ramblings of a couple of black elites. But I would submit that this brief exchange is indicative of a larger uplift narrative that celebrates black "achievement" at the expense of black folks who, like my grandmother, either failed to do or simply *did not desire to do* what it would have taken for them to become firmly entrenched within the ranks of the black bourgeoisie (aka "bougie") or the "upwardly mobile."[11]

The final reason I believe the telling of Grammy's story is important is because, rather than being seen merely as the relics of a bygone era whose lives have no bearing on the lives of post–civil rights black women other than as historical lore, our grandmothers, mothers, and othermothers help us to reckon with what it means to live wholly and completely, *in spite of.* To speak of black social life is to speak of this radical capacity to live—to live deeply righteous lives even in the midst of all that brings death close or, as Lucille Clifton puts it, to celebrate "everyday / something has tried to kill me / and has failed."[12] It is to affirm the "tragicomic confrontation with life" that characterizes so much of black humanity and to assert "those qualities which are of value beyond any question of segregation, economics or previous conditions of servitude."[13] Black social life is, fundamentally, the register of black experience that is not reducible to the terror that calls it into existence but is the rich remainder, the multifaceted artifact of black communal resistance and resilience that is expressed in black idioms, cultural forms, traditions, and ways of being.

For all that Ellison gets charged with elitism and racial neglect, his writings and commentary forcefully reveal something of this form of life I am concerned with addressing, and it is perhaps best revealed in an interview he gave to Richard Stern in 1961. Upon being asked by Stern when he "became conscious that there was something precious about being a Negro in this country at this time," Ellison told the story of a cotton patch. He reminisced on the period of his childhood in Oklahoma when some children would have to leave school periodically to work in the cotton fields with their parents. Although this was work most parents fervently wished they did not have to do and did not want for their children, he remembered being envious of those children who went away to the cotton fields. For Ellison realized the significance of what those children came home with, which was about something other than the odious conditions under which they and their families labored.

> And it wasn't the hard work which they stressed, but the communion, the playing, the eating, the dancing and the singing. And they brought back jokes, our Negro jokes—not those told about Negroes by whites—and they always returned with Negro folk stories which I'd never heard before and which couldn't be found in any books I knew about. This was something to affirm and I felt there was a richness in it. I didn't think too much about it, but what my schoolmates shared in the country and what I felt in their accounts of it—it seemed much more real than the Negro middle-class values which were taught in school.[14]

Later in that same interview Ellison refers to the black barbershop as the place where one could find "more unself-conscious affirmation ... on a Saturday than you can find in a Negro college in a month." And later still, he talks about how the "Negro farm people" who visited Tuskegee University during graduation week while he was a student there would skip out on the "big-shot word artists ... making their most impressive speeches" during the commencement exercises in order to visit and celebrate among themselves on the athletic fields. It was these "festivals" Ellison would sneak off to watch because he "found their unrhetorical activities on the old football field the more meaningful."[15]

The cotton field, the barbershop, and the athletic field. In Ellison's day and in our own, these and other places like them that we could name—the hair salon, the front porch, the church basement, the street corner, the backyard barbecue, the house party, the kitchen table—are where black social life fulfills its greatest potential. These places where everyday, ordinary, or what John Langston Gwaltney's respondents might call "drylongso," black folks gather together in the name of perhaps nothing more than *themselves* are fundamental to reckoning with "that same pain and that same pleasure" that constitutes blackness.[16] And so my concern here is to think about how these gatherings are extended across the terrain of black female experience and made legible by black women's lives and bodies in the making of a sociality that is firmly rooted in the black imaginary.

BLACK SOCIAL LIFE

My discussion of black social life here is intentionally at odds with social death theory, or theoretical positions that posit black life as little more than a vestige of slavery and therefore largely uninhabitable or degraded and thus something to be "escaped" in one way or another. Under this line of reasoning, the escape artists turn out to be those Exceptional Negroes who are successfully able to throw off the shackles of nihilism and defeatism and whatever other "isms" plague the black masses in order to become exemplary citizens who are, within the logics of black achievement, "credits" to the race—so that "the race" ostensibly becomes something other than what it is, something that is at a remove from its genesis, something that is defined *against* those entities that or who are critical to its very existence.

This fleecing of black life takes multiple forms and occurs in any number of different locations both within and beyond academia. First, it is at the heart of the revulsion to the ghetto, people who inhabit the ghetto, and people who supposedly "act" ghetto.[17] As David Wellman explains, this revulsion in everyday interactions among lay black people and black social critics à la Bill Cosby, Alvin Poussaint, Orlando Patterson, and Juan Williams, as well as among black neoconservatives such as Thomas Sowell, John McWhorter, and Shelby Steele, is often situated today within the rhetoric of "personal responsibility" and is out of alignment with "an abundance of evidence [that] has been generated over the past couple of decades which credibly argues that neither culture nor personal deficiencies cause the problems that haunt inner cities."[18] Wellman goes on to outline the assumptions that undergird this rhetoric:

> They assume the "underclass" is largely an African American formation found in inner cities; that it subscribes to a value system at odds with both mainstream American sentiments and middle-class Black culture; that it is poor because households are headed by females and males who refuse to work. They also assume that male criminal behavior in combination with female dependency on welfare are powerful deterrents to gainful employment. As a result, they suppose, the work ethic has been subverted and moral order has collapsed in the inner cities. They think access to employment opportunity structures is available to qualified applicants regardless of residence or race, and joblessness in inner cities

is therefore the result of deficient motivation, self-esteem, or education. They also believe inner cities are isolated from the communities that surround them and that, complicating matters, the tensions between inner-city gangs and their neighborhoods divide these two groups.[19]

These "folk theories of social identity" that Wellman convincingly shows are riddled with conceptual and methodological defects and are largely debunked by ethnographic research thus do not reveal any actionable causes of sustained black poverty, "underachievement," or "failure."[20] They are instead used in the service of a class-based distancing of the "good" blacks from the "bad" blacks that thereby absolves the "good" or "respectable" blacks of any collective responsibility for attending to the real causes of black suffering or of black *middle-class* decline, disciplines and further stigmatizes those individuals who do not act in accordance with normative middle-class values, and buffers themselves against that same stigma.

The degradation of black social life also occurs by way of discourses that hold that social problems plaguing black communities (gang violence, what gets referred to as "black-on-black crime," illicit drug use, teenage pregnancy, etc.) and particular cultural practices and traditions (hair straightening and the use of hair extensions, gangsta rap, wearing baggy clothing, the prohibition against "acting white," use of the word "nigga," etc.) are primarily the consequences of low self-esteem and the internalization of negative stereotypes among black people. These are certainly factors in some cases and for some people, but there is evidence to suggest such claims are often largely overstated and/or fail to consider viable alternative readings. For example, John Jackson uses the term "ghetto fabulous" in his inventive ethnographic study of Harlem residents to refer to the "embrace [of] a sense of self utterly irreducible to one's assumed location at the residential and spatial bottom of national or international pecking orders. Ghetto fabulousness takes the quantified assumptions of localized marginality and transforms them into a qualitatively different kind of lived experience."[21] For Jackson, the knock-off consumerism of black people living in poor and underresourced communities cannot be explained away as rote materialism and excess on the behalf of people who can little afford it and who should consequently be directing their attentions elsewhere but is a creative articulation of life at the margins and a rejection of the pathologization of ghetto life.

In another instance Kobena Mercer takes issue "with the widespread argument that, because it involves straightening, the curly-perm hairstyle represents either a wretched imitation of white people's hair or, what amounts to the same thing, a diseased state of black consciousness."[22] Though he references a hairstyle that is by now largely out of fashion, the larger point Mercer makes remains valid and could very well be rearticulated in reference to the more contemporary conversations happening around natural hair care.[23] That is, he argues the need to "depsychologize" hair straightening and other black hairstyles, recognizing them as aesthetic cultural practices that hold social and symbolic meaning, rather than being merely evidence of rampant self-loathing and inferiority complexes among black people. He goes on to discuss how, historically, "natural" styles such as the Afro and (dread)locks have been used in the service of a romanticized "counterhegemonic tactic of inversion" that fails to actually invoke the connection to Africa such hairstyles are often meant or understood to signal.[24] Similarly, Robin Kelley situates the Afro within the historical context out of which it emerged, noting its origins as a mod fashion statement in bourgeois high society that was subsequently commodified in the marketplace in the 1960s and 1970s as a signifier of "soul." The ultimate point, Kelley contends, is that by overinterpreting black cultural practices like hairstyling as if they are political treatises, "the stylistic and aesthetic conventions that render the form and performance more attractive than the message" are missed, and the meaning of such practices to the actual people who engage them are disregarded or misinterpreted.[25]

A final example of an alternative reading of purported black pathology is Gwen Bergner's discussion of the doll experiments conducted by Kenneth and Mamie Clark that were used to buttress the *Brown v. Board of Education* ruling handed down by the Supreme Court in 1954. The Clarks' study famously found that when given the choice between a brown doll and a white doll, black children tended to identify with the brown doll but ultimately chose the white doll as the "nice" one and the one they preferred to play with. The Clarks ultimately concluded that this preference meant black children had internalized negative societal messages regarding blackness and therefore suffered from damaged self-esteems. Although the Clark doll experiments have been discredited on methodological grounds by researchers since at least the late 1960s, they and their progeny continue to be used as evidence to support the widespread notion that black people as a group suffer from low self-esteem due to racism.[26] Yet, as Bergner notes, later racial preference tests that controlled for factors the Clarks did not consider, such as region, sex, class, age, and the interviewer's race, produced contradictory results, and these results suggest the purported link between racial identity and self-esteem is precarious at best.[27]

Black social life is also impugned when social programs such as affirmative action, WIC, food stamps, and welfare are targeted for reduction or elimination in the name of "color-blind" policies meant to encourage "self-help"—which is but another formulation of personal responsibility aimed at marginalized communities, people of color in particular. Here again, these anguished calls for self-help are premised on assumptions about black people that do not actually bear themselves out but are good for making scapegoats of the most vulnerable. Ange-Marie Hancock, for example, notes how welfare queen mythology influenced the development and eventual passage of the 1996 Personal Responsibility and Work Opportunity Act that was supposed to "reform" welfare but has subsequently had devastating consequences for welfare recipients—most of whom are *not* black.[28] Likewise, Dorothy Roberts notes how this same deviant black mother mythology has influenced governmental policies affecting black women's reproductive capacities historically, including the coerced and involuntary sterilizations of black women that occurred throughout the twentieth century and the disparate treatment of black women in prosecutions of drug-addicted mothers.[29]

There is yet another strand of black social death theory that is loosely organized around the notion of "antiblackness" or "afro-pessimism," which, per Frank Wilderson, essentially claims that "Blackness is both that outside which makes it possible for White and non-White (i.e., Asians and Latinos) positions to exist and, simultaneously, contest existence." As such, "the structure of the entire world's semantic field . . . is sutured by anti-Black solidarity."[30] Afro-pessimists are skeptical both of multiculturalism, which they feel does not have the capacity to respond meaningfully or coherently to white supremacy, and of solution-oriented responses to black suffering, because they potentially negate the terror of that suffering.[31] It is not enough to say that black people are alienated or degraded or oppressed because, for them, blackness occupies the terrain of the noncommunicable and is predicated on "modalities of accumulation and fungibility," or an absolute negation.[32] In other words, black people are *not* subaltern subjects but nonhuman nonbeings whose very existence is predicated on death and violence. That said, black social death as the afro-pessimists conceive of it cannot be neatly summed up as the opposite of black social life. According to Jared Sexton,

> Black optimism is not the negation of the negation that is afro-pessimism, just as black social life does not negate black social death by inhabiting and vitalizing it. A living death is as much a death as it is a living. Nothing in afro-pessimism suggests that there is no black (social) life, only that black life is not social life in the universe formed by the codes of state and civil society, of citizen and subject, of nation and culture, or people and place, of history and heritage, of all the things that colonial society has in common with the colonized, of all that capital has in common with labor—the modern world system. Black life is not lived in the world that the world lives in, but is lived underground, in outer space. . . . Black life is not social, or rather . . . black life is *lived* in social *death*. Double emphasis, on lived and on death.[33]

Sexton's point is well taken, and afro-pessimism as it is synopsized by him and others goes a long way toward helping us understand, even reconceptualize, the mandate of blackness. Indeed, throughout this book I call on several theorists whose work is situated along this particular trajectory of thought to help me make my own case for blackness. Yet where I ultimately depart from the afro-pessimist position is in this concern over "the modern world system" that Sexton so carefully, and I think rightly, delineates. Here I am not concerned as much with thinking about how black social life is ordered according to "the universe formed by the codes of state and civil society" and so forth as I am with thinking about how social life is defined wholly within the parameters of what Hortense Spillers has called in reference to black communal relations the "intramural,"[34] what Elizabeth Alexander refers to in her discussion of "black life and creativity behind the public face of stereotype" as the "black interior,"[35] and what Toni Morrison calls "interior life."[36] To put a finer point on it, whether "the world" thinks my grandmother and mother and all those folks who live on the South Side of Peoria and the South Side of Chicago and every other hood and ghetto and community and street where black folks gather are "fungible" or not, I want to think about what those folks think about themselves because, in so doing, I am able to consider black social life from the vantage point at which it is lived, rather than at which it is merely viewed or policed or looked in on occasionally.[37] This is meant not to deny the force of the world order on black sociality but to take the view that the way black people go about making themselves, both because of and regardless of the conditions of their making, their *own* world order, is as appropriate and necessary a starting place as any other.

This, again, is an Ellisonian formulation. Ellison's ideological disagreements with his one-time mentor Richard Wright are well known, and in his essay "The World and the Jug" Ellison critiques Wright's most famous work, *Native Son*, because it begins "with the ideological proposition that what whites think of the Negro's reality is more important than what Negroes themselves know it to be."[38] The apparent concern of Ellison's writing was not to somehow "prove" or reinforce how devastating and tragic black life is or is claimed to be but to express the complexity of black life in all of its fullness according to his own experience of it and the experiences of those black folks who were committed to living it according to their own standards and sense of regard for themselves. And so it is from this line of thinking that *Scandalize My Name: Black Feminist Practice and the Making of Black Social Life* emerges.

BLACKNESS AND REPRESENTATION

While the specter of representation looms large over this project, my entry point into thinking about representation is guided by my interest in the interplay between the intramural (black community) and the interior (black self). My focus is consequently turned inside out, having less to do with how black social life is represented than with what the conditions of black social life reveal about the terms of representation itself. *Scandalize My Name* is thus an inquiry into the *representability* of black social life primarily by way of poor and working-class black women and the narratives that have come to define them in public culture. But rather than assume the offensiveness or incoherence of said narratives—angry, strong, oversexed, hyperreligious, deviant—or question why black women are represented in particular ways, I consider how the logics of representation, coded by terms such as "value," "visibility," "citizenship," "morality," "respectability," and "responsibility," *necessarily* fail to account for the reality of black lived experience. Accordingly, the primary issue is not to determine whether particular representations are more or less accurate or inaccurate but to suggest that black social life defies the limitations of representational discourse and practice.

Because I am more interested in thinking about how black women live in, through, and outside of the markers of black female identity that have come to define them publicly than I am with how other people who are not black women respond to those markers, I am less interested in a foray into what I refer to as *stereotype discourse*. As discussed here, stereotype discourse is the preoccupation with locating pathology or righteousness in certain cultural actors or texts that, in this context, often functions to position black female iconography along a continuum of "positive" or "negative" representations, sometimes even when it explicitly purports to do otherwise. Although there has been much scholarly talk about the need to move beyond the good/bad binary at least since Stuart Hall called for the end of the "essential black subject" in the late 1980s, and despite the fact that it's been more than twenty years since Herman Gray argued that "no longer can our analyses be burdened unnecessarily by the weight of an eternal search for either 'authentic' media representations of 'blackness' or accurate reflections of African American social and cultural life,"[39] very often discussions about black female representation in public culture— news and social media, film and televisual texts, political discourses, and the like—continue to revolve around these same divides, both in popular media commentary and in academic work. Accordingly, this work tends to get so mired in "archetype-hunting,"[40] the seemingly endless practice of naming how this or that image or representation conforms to this or that foregoing stereotype of black people, that it essentially becomes counterproductive. These critics become so invested in saying what black people are not—they are *not* angry, they are *not* lazy, they are *not* violent, they are *not* hypersexual—that it becomes difficult to fathom who black people *are*, other than, perhaps, the inverse of every negative thing that has ever been said about them. And I suppose *that* is a project, but it is not mine.

To be sure, much of the writing and thinking about black female representation has concentrated on the still deeply entrenched stereotypes of black women for good reason, and the concerns that leading black female scholars have had over the historical legacies and continued replication of tropes like the asexual Mammy, the sharp-tongued Sapphire, the tragic mulatto, and the hypersexual Jezebel have been foundational in situating black women within the matrix of U.S. sociopolitical thought and practice. It is, in fact, what initiated my own interest in this work and has been critical in helping me to situate myself as a U.S. black woman. *But for* the formidable work that scholars such as Deborah Gray White, Trudier Harris, Patricia Hill Collins, bell hooks, Dorothy Roberts, Patricia Turner, Michele Wallace, and others have done in naming the various ways black women's bodies and lives have been constructed/construed in the national mythos via the previously named tropes and their derivatives, my project could not exist at all. My challenge, then, is to extend this work in a way that responds to the exigencies of the current moment but is not overdetermined by the concerns that made such work necessary in the first place.

My argument about the inability of representation to account for black social life is a move in this direction and is occasioned at least in part by Wilderson's discussion of the black subject, that is, the slave, in American civil society, which he refers to as "a scandal at the level of discourse" who "emerge[s] as the unthought."[41] Wilderson contends that Marxism, particularly as it is conceptualized by Antonio Gramsci in *Prison Notebooks*, assumes a black subject, a worker, that cannot in fact exist because "whereas the positionality of the worker enables the reconfiguration of civil society, the positionality of the slave exists as a destabilizing force within civil society because civil society gains its coherence, *the very tabula raza upon which workers and industrialists struggle for hegemony*, through the violence of black erasure."[42] Because black chattel slavery inaugurated U.S. capitalism and U.S. civil society is consequently predicated on the intersection of capitalism and white supremacy, the slave does not enter into the transactions of value but is instead "an articulation of a despotic irrationality [white supremacy] whereas the worker is an articulation of a symbolic rationality [capitalism]."[43] For Wilderson, the primary referent of blackness is death, and the black subject position threatens the assumptive logic of Gramscian discourse. From the perspective taken here, however, blackness cannot be aligned with death because black social life, the *primary* measure of black subjectivity, is, as Sexton suggests, fugitive—it coheres, accumulates its sociality, in the wild. Black social life is therefore irreducible to the codes of (white) civil society that it brings into being; the *outside* of value is *its* tabula raza.

That point of distinction aside, Wilderson's critical discussion of the unthought black subject, or what Ntozake Shange calls "the unconscious of the entire Western world,"[44] makes way for my consideration of the black woman who both is and causes a scandal within the field of representation. Consequently, what I want to posit is the contemplation of a black female subjectivity that attains meaning by way of an *amoral* social order that exists beyond the dichotomous regulatory regimes that structure so much of representational discourse. My ultimate concern is with thinking about how representation accounts for, or fails to account for as the case may be, a form of life that, "on the one hand, *is not what it is* and, on the other hand, is irreducible to what it is used for."[45] That is to say, while I do not disagree about the existence of problematic stereotypes of black women, I want to suggest that the problem is not one that can be gotten at by refuting the stereotype itself. Instead, the stereotype reveals the problem; it is, in fact, an artifact of the problem, which is not the wrongness or rightness of any particular black person or persons or their societal representations but the inability of representational discourse to contend with the unthought black subject who destabilizes "civil society" and, consequently, the very notion of civility itself.[46]

Framed in this way, what it means to *think* can neither be underestimated nor taken for granted, since, as we know from Hannah Arendt, "thinking itself is such a dangerous enterprise."[47] To think about the unthought is to clear space for the question, for "questioning as ritual, questioning as exploration rather than the search for certainty."[48] It is about the refinement of the question and deliberation in ways that do not always lead to neat conclusions or demonstrable solutions. And, finally, it is affirmation of and solidarity with a way of life that is not beholden to the mandates, constraints, or allegiances of academic discourse and practice. *Scandalize My Name* is thus a sustained thought experiment that takes as its premise the irreducible sociality of black life. It contends that black social life is the eschewal and critique of the affliction of privilege that resides in the preoccupation with the individual self. It transforms the principal complaint of stereotype discourse—that the stereotype comes to stand for all of us—into the grounds on which to enact a radical engagement with the self that cannot be itself alone.[49] And it asserts that what it means to be with and for black people is not the evisceration of the ego but the recognition that there is and can be no "post" to blackness because blackness is what calls our individual and collective selves into being.[50]

This brings me, at last, to the question of methodology. To get at this question, I first return to the work of Hortense Spillers, who more than twenty years ago argued the need for a "cultural demography" in which the meaning and experience of "home" and "community" would be newly, or uniquely, theorized within black studies:

> If African-American culture has been transformed by internal divisions of flight and dispersal—and the latter must also mean various *repositionings* in the national culture and not simple, physical movement, or mobility, alone—then the object of analysis must be grasped in light of it.
>
> But the intellectual has imagined flight only in its negative instance as a supposed rejection, when his very status, or standing, *as an intellectual* requires that he take on a language and disposition that are "foreign." In other words, the work of the academy, or more specifically, the "cognitive apparatus," is defined, symbolically speaking, as "not-mother," a "not-my-own." I am referring less to the maternal and paternal objects here as gendered actants of precisely defined sexual role than as the *ground of intimacy* that the subject *assumes*: the more or less harmonious ensemble of impressions that bound me not only to my body, but my body as it is reflected back to me in the eyes of others that I recognize *as like myself.* Whether or not this relation is troubled is less the point than that its complexities convey to one the sense of ease—the relay of constitutive continuities among particular kinetic, linguistic, sensual, and material gestures—through which one comes to experience home. From this point of view, community describes both the extension of home as well as its spatial/temporal genesis. As I understand it, community, however, is already a *cross-weave*—its local economisms linked into a larger network of sociopolitical/cultural relations and the messages that traverse it consequently—that prepares its subjects to receive the supplemental. We cannot imagine learning, acquisition, the *foreign* language, precisely as the various pains of intrusion unless we first understand how community has intimately prepared the ground as the apparent continuing unity against which "unhome" is measured.[51]

In sum, Spillers asserts the critical significance of contemplating dispersal in black studies, where dispersal is distinguished both from flight, or the pathological desire to flee or reject one's community, and the physical movement away from home. Here dispersal refers to what it means to "leave home to learn to remember,"[52] physically and otherwise, and the various ways in which the community prepares us for, and is transformed by, our leave-taking. The community is thus "my primary speech,"[53] an "internal diaspora"[54] to which it is not necessary to "go back" because it is always with me wherever I go. And what this "going" requires is that I have the capacity to perceive community neither as a dereliction in need of a "representative hero" nor as an undifferentiated mass bereft of critical thought but as a "layering of negotiable differences" that informs and shapes the work I do.[55]

Since I have left or, more precisely, *because* I have left my natal community for the "cognitive apparatus," this primary concern that Spillers enumerates with attending to where and how one is *from* constitutes the scaffolding of this text. I consequently engage a form of storytelling, what I consider to be the consummate methodology and an outcome and condition of black social life—the craft of which is honed by way of various rhetorical occasions within the black life-world that include, among others, signifyin', shooting the shit, playing the dozens, lyin', testifying, and testilyin'.[56] Because I recognize storytelling as "the way human beings organize their human knowledge"[57] and because it has been so essential in my own coming to knowledge, from the anecdotal wisdom of my grandmother to the ever-evolving tall tales of my dad and his brothers to the bedtime stories my mother read to me right up until I anointed myself too old for such things, I privilege it here as a way of comprehending the "negotiable differences" that are so fundamental to black life.

The methodological practice I occasion here, aside from its roots in communal and familial storytelling, is most readily referred to in academe as "autoethnography," or "the method and product of researching and writing about personal lived experiences and their relationship to culture."[58] Autoethnography is most firmly established as a practice in the social sciences, anthropology in particular, but I use it as the staging ground of my inquiries here because of its usefulness in thinking through "the bigger story,"[59] which in the case at hand is the (re)conceptualization of community as an "object of knowledge"[60] that has something critically important to tell us about the conditions of black sociality. I am quite clear that my own experience as a black, female, working-class Peoria native turned academic is a singular experience that cannot adequately stand in for any other. Victor Anderson, for example, relates a very different experience of home, one no less significant than my own, that reminds us of the terror and ambiguity that can and does accompany the notion of home and its auxiliaries for many people, and Kimberlé Crenshaw, among others, outlines the threat home too often poses for women, particularly women of color, who are subject to routinized violence as a *consequence* of home.[61] Still, in the vein of Toni Morrison, who contends that discourses about race are ultimately discourses about home and the "devastations, pleasures, and imperatives of homelessness" as manifested across a range of subject formations,[62] I offer up this experience as a sort of ideological sight line, a way of thinking the place and project of home and all of its enabling (and disabling) conditions, not the least of which are black women, in the making of black social life.

I begin this inquiry in chapter 1 with a discussion of anger. Here I am interested neither in contextualizing anger as a positive mechanism for feminist engagement nor in disavowing it as antithetical to the feminist cause but in considering what staking a claim for anger might reveal about black female subjectivity. "Getting Happy," chapter 2, uses two significant moments in the black Christian life-world—the outing of gospel singer Tonéx and the phenomenon that was Juanita Bynum's "No More Sheets" sermon—to get at the socioreligious meaning and significance of those whom James Baldwin references as "God's decoys." Chapter 3, "The Way It Is," uses the moment of an in-home bachelorette party to stage a discussion about what Daphne Brooks calls "black feminist surrogation"[63] and posits the R&B singer as a key surrogate figure in contemplating the contours of black women's social intimacy. In "Baby Mama," chapter 4, I use the black teenage mother and the rhetoric of pathology surrounding her, particularly as it played out in the pages of Peoria's newspaper, the *Journal Star*, in 1994, to enable a discussion about what Lindon Barrett refers to as the "spectre of bla(n)ckness."[64] Finally, in chapter 5, "In the Life," I discuss the deaths of eight black women that occurred at the hands of a Peoria-area serial killer between 2003 and 2004. I end here because the relay between violence and value that structures that discussion is the off-ramp to a whole range of further discussions yet to be completed about black feminist practice, black social life, and what it means to be with and for black people.

1

ON ANGER

> We lived on Sidell Ave. until 1936. The only thing I can remember about being on Sidell is when my brother Nate was teasing me. I got angry and hit him in the temple with a fork. I had a terrible temper.
>
> —*A BRIEF AUTOBIOGRAPHY OF BERNICE L. TURNER*

Like my grandmother before me I have been well acquainted with anger my entire life. In her case, it was her older brother, my Uncle Nate, who felt the fullest extent of her wrath, while in my case it was my younger brother, Rufus Jr., who was the most likely recipient of my, shall we say, "displays of temperament" growing up. (Of course, some of this has to do with the fact that siblings are the perfect built-in scapegoats. Who better to project every complicated adolescent feeling onto than someone your parents—who are often the real source of your anger but whom, at least the way I grew up, you could not freely express that to—are going to force to love you no matter what?). Still, it wasn't until I was in my midtwenties that I first began trying to comprehend my vexed and often perplexing relationship with anger as something more than reactionary (and, ironically, often *angry*) disavowal. At the time, I was peripherally involved with someone, a black man, who after I told him about my interest in writing on the topic of black women and anger told me that I should not write about said topic because I am "too close" to it. As the argument went, I would not have any veracity if I attempted an argument about angry black women because I am myself an angry black woman, or I would at least be perceived as such by anyone who engaged my work. I should leave all that angry black woman talk to someone else, someone not black and female. Now, I would like to tell you that my response to homeboy was to run down the whole history of black women being deemed unverifiable and his ill extension of that line of thinking, that I told him that thing Audre Lorde said about black women not needing others to speak for us and referred him to Patricia Hill Collins's discussion of the significance of black women's thinking about themselves[1]—except that I really don't remember what I said, and I'm pretty sure I didn't give him the telling off he might, by all rights, have deserved. I suppose I didn't want him to think I was angry.

While hindsight offers up a range of responses to provocations of this sort, I'm not as much interested in a feminist takedown of my would-be provocateur as I am with thinking about the notion of *proximity* that his "advice" occasioned: *What does it mean to be "too close" to anger? How can it be that the nearness of a thing puts it beyond reach? What are the particularities of anger such that its nearness, its acquaintanceship with black female personality, is so vexed as to be potentially impracticable or illegible?*

My initial interest in thinking about black women and anger in a sustained way came about as a consequence of reality television. Or, rather, reality television was the initial site where I saw black women's anger being taken up substantively. I was a law student in 2004 when Omarosa Manigault (then Manigault-Stallworth), the angry black woman par excellence, hit the reality television scene. I knew nothing of her or the show she helped popularize until my father's youngest sister, my Aunt Sweet, called me all worked up about this black woman on *The Apprentice* who was *taking names*. She brokered no fools, she asserted herself without apology, she was undeterred by the discomfort her presence caused others, and what made her especially attractive to my aunt, she was well educated and capable of thriving within a corporate environment—she'd been in graduate school at Howard University and had worked for the Clinton administration before her stint on *The Apprentice*. By the time I finally tuned in, primarily due to my aunt's urging, Omarosa was being "fired" from the show after having caused all manner of disruption and being deemed difficult to work with by her teammates—an assessment that, frankly, was not hard to understand. Yet what I came to know as my dalliance with reality television evolved into study is that those early days of Omarosa's infamy are significant in marking a distinction between the angry black woman she *was* and the angry black woman she *became*. Omarosa claimed her cutthroat "strategy" of remaining cold and calculating and not forming personal relationships with her teammates was an effect of her competitive drive and not the entirety of her personality, as she contended was played up by the show to her detriment. That said, she quickly parlayed her failed bid to become the apprentice into a successful career as a reality television personality largely on the strength of her ability to, in her words, "capitalize" on and "exploit" the "naughty girl" image she cultivated by way of *The Apprentice*. When asked about the claim by one of her fellow contestants, a white man, that the show had made him into a commodity, she countered, "I wouldn't empower anyone to treat me like a commodity. Sure [producer] Mark Burnett did the editing, and America saw what it saw, but I marketed and packaged the character that's become Omarosa."[2]

These simultaneously dueling and *dualing* performances of the angry black woman—one that emerges simply as a consequence of being a competitive black woman who is "not here to make friends" and the other that is a deliberate economic strategy—are at the heart of the debate over the authenticity or *realness* of reality television and its relationship to black women. I became particularly attuned to this debate as I watched the proliferation of reality television at the turn of the twenty-first century and, consequently, the growth of angry black womandom, from *America's Next Top Model* (2003–15), which always had at least one, and usually more than one, angry black woman on each successive cycle, to BET's *College Hill* (2004–9), which, to the chagrin of many black people, helped inaugurate the angry black woman on black network television, to *Flavor of Love* (2006–8) and its progeny, which gave us any number of angry black women but none more divisive or *entertaining* than Tiffany "New York" Pollard, who became the first black woman to star on her own reality show spin-off. What I quickly noted was an appreciable and completely relevant concern about to what extent the *behind*-the-scenes production affects the way women on these and similarly styled shows behave *on* screen and whether the angry black woman is but another product of corporate interests that comes at the expense of black folks—even if, as in the case of Omarosa, some black people are involved in and benefit from the arrangement.

In the ensuing years since my initial foray into reality television, and as the genre has come to dominate television programming, the angry black woman has also become, in all of her neck-swiveling, punch-throwing, tongue-lashing glory, a favorite whipping girl of black cultural commentators of all stripes—from print and television journalists to armchair critics and academics to reality-television personalities themselves. Several years after my Aunt Sweet unwittingly helped inaugurate my interest in black women on reality television, which I continued to cultivate upon entering graduate school, I temporarily went to live with her and her two then-teenage daughters during a fellowship leave. I finally had other people, black women no less, to watch television with again. But by this time black reality television, that is, reality shows that feature primarily black casts and target black audiences, had become both a programming mainstay and par-ticular target of black animus, and my aunt had joined the ranks of those who could not abide the behavior of black people, and (angry) black women in particular, on "those shows" (leaving aside for the moment that more than once it was my aunt who caught *me* up on the goings on of *The Real Housewives of Atlanta*), while my own position had morphed from disin-terest to dis-ease to something bordering on compulsion. Although it is not my intention here to go into an exposition of black women's complex rela-tionship with reality television—a relationship that is ultimately rooted in an extensive history that transcends the form[3]—I do want to briefly outline the concerns of my aunt and many others regarding the *presence* of black women on reality television that help occasion the current discussion.

The arguments made against the angry black woman of reality television typically fall into one of three modes of "stereotype discourse," or the con-cern over whether particular mediated images or texts, one, conform to foregoing, historically contingent, stereotypes of black people and, two, correspond to the lives and experiences of those they potentially stand in for or purport to represent. According to the *protectionist mode* of stereo-type discourse, the angry black woman is a problem because she makes black folks, particularly black women, look bad. As heir apparent of the noxious Sapphire, whose embodiment in the form of one Ernestine Wade was eventually, and inevitably, expelled from television by the presumptive leaders of the race, the angry black woman must also be done away with in order to protect against the (further) denigration of blackness. Conse-quently, petitions are sometimes circulated and letters are sometimes writ-ten demanding certain shows or cast members deemed offensive be taken off the air in the name of the greater good. Alternatively, those whose think-ing is more in alignment with the *additive mode* argue that the primary problem with the angry black woman is that she is the *dominant* represen-tation of black women. Thus the solution is not to attempt to petition away every image of every angry black woman but to introduce other images of black women that can broaden out black female representation. Finally, adherents to the *reformative mode*, which may or may not work in conjunction with either of the other two modes, suggest the problem is that black women's anger is misunderstood. The angry black woman is ultimately a misrepresentation of black women's *authentic* anger, which at the very least is the consequence of their continued racial and sexual marginalization. Under this mode the angry black woman has the potential to be useful but only if properly contextualized as the outcome of black women's justifiable anger at the conditions of their lives.

Despite the different approaches, within each mode of stereotype discourse, whether protectionist, additive, or reformative, the angry black woman represents an immoral sociality that must be abolished, diluted, or reformulated—that is, *made distant* in one way or another—in order for black female representation, and ultimately black women, to attain positive value. But what might it mean to refuse positivity, to refuse to back away from or *alter* anger, to consider anger neither as righteous nor as detriment but as *critical posture*? That is to say, what if rather than starting from the position of denial, we start from the position of *claim*? To take up anger in this way is an anxiety-producing proposition, in the first place, because it risks being misunderstood either as complicity with an all-too-common reductionism of black female behavior as pathological deviance or as an excuse for that same alleged deviance. But the second and more immediate reason it initially invoked my own anxiety has to do with something Lorde wrote about in her own discussion of "our angers":

> But by and large, we avoid open expression of them, or cordon them off in a rigid and unapproachable politeness. The rage that feels illicit or unjustified is kept secret, unnamed, and preserved forever. We are stuffed with furies, against ourselves, against each other, terrified to examine them lest we find ourselves in bold print fingered and named what we have always felt and even sometimes preferred ourselves to be—alone.[4]

Accordingly, what it means for me to take up anger as critical posture is to take up *myself* and, even more importantly, my relationship to other black women. The angst is not that I do not have the capacity to write about black women's anger or even that I will be taken for an angry black woman but that I am never *not* taken for an angry black woman, and I know instinctively that excavating the meaning and consequence of this taken-ness requires something more than defense. While the angry black woman is by no means a new millennium formulation, her presence on reality tele-vision newly exposes the raw nerve that is the juncture between black women and anger, and I suspect that it is precisely because of my own po-sitionality that I have had some difficulty accessing the "something more" in the face of this exposure. I am experienced in stereotype discourse. I am trained to recognize the residue of particular historical formulations of black female identity and to use my "platform" to call out any depictions that conform to this undoubtedly racist, sexist history. It is a necessary training, without which I could not have authored this text, among any number of other activities essential to my personal and professional liveli-hood. But it is also a training that neither begins nor ends in the academy and is supplemented by my external or *other* experience. Yet the dismissal and denigration of this experience, which is fundamentally rooted in my relationship to the place and people I come from, my natal community, is often the prerequisite for and outcome of "higher" learning.

The effects of this disengagement are readily apparent in the varying conversations I have had over the years with black people about reality tele-vision. Almost without exception, when I have conversations with academ-ics or other people, like my aunt, who are invested in certain academic protocols even if they do not labor within the academy itself, talk quickly turns to representation (How does this form make us look?), production (How "real" is this form, and who is responsible for it?), and the conse-quences of the intersections between the two. I have often found these to be compelling and useful conversations from which I have learned a great deal. They are also often shrouded in disclaimer: if these individuals watch reality television at all, and often they claim not to, there are limits to what they will watch or it is merely as "guilty pleasure" or "escapism" and not something they take at all seriously. In contrast, when I have conversations with other people, usually friends and family members in informal settings, who are less indebted or exposed to "the cultures of the learned,"[5] they may have similar concerns about representation and production, but these con-cerns are more usually asides to the primary conversation, which tend to have more to do with the substance of the thing under consideration—the plots, the relationships between characters, their own personal connection to or feelings about the plots and characters—than with the conditions or effects of their making. I have also found these to be compelling and useful conversations from which I have learned a lot, and because people in this latter group are generally less concerned with critiquing the form than the content, they are better equipped to attend to the *essence* of black women's anger than the categorization, qualification, or legislation of the angry black woman. That is to say, they are more likely to *assume* the relationship between black women and anger without consequently naming anger as something from which black women should necessarily hold themselves apart. This often shows up in conversations about what black women will and won't take, how they do and do not behave, and in response to the actions of angry black women on television. Ironically, my Aunt Sweet's early embrace of Omarosa is indicative of this disposition. Even though she eventually distanced herself, at least theoretically, from reality television, Omarosa's resilient, take-no-shit demeanor initially resonated with my aunt, who knows firsthand what it is to survive corporate America as a black woman. She intuitively understood Omarosa and appreciated the opportunity to witness another black woman boldly navigating the same implicit and explicit hostilities she had experienced in her own career, even if that opportunity did come via a highly produced television show meant purely for entertainment and (someone else's) economic gain.

I would consequently argue that what eventually turned my aunt off from reality television was not the anger of black women per se but the betrayal of a certain kind of containment strategy. Black women can exhibit anger or its corollaries—bitterness, animosity, frigidity, hostility, and the like—but only when mitigated by manner(s), education, proper speech, and so on, and only when that anger has to do with something virtuous like career, family (values), or opposition to racist discrimination. But anger that takes the form of unadulterated *act-up*—brawling, yelling, cursing, going off—or has to do with something as "insignificant" as a baby daddy or a rivalry with another woman is wholly out of bounds. Though there is a critique to be made of this position, my point here is neither to critique the position nor my aunt but to think through what my aunt's position enables. And that is, namely, that there is something to be said for black women's anger that cannot be said solely by way of disavowal.

At the outset of *Red, White, and Black*, Frank Wilderson tells the story of a "crazy" black woman who, when he was a student at Columbia University in New York, used to stand outside the university gate and yell at nonblack people as they entered that they had stolen her sofa and sold her into slavery. She would wink at her black passersby, and they would not wink back, either, as Wilderson claims, out of a sense that the woman's rhetoric was out of step with their notions of racial justice or out of fear that her isolated state might be somehow communicable. Wilderson uses the story of this "crazy" black woman as the opening onto a thesis about what he calls the structure of U.S. racial antagonisms. This thesis essentially holds that despite the fact that social upheaval is typically conceptualized as conflict, "i.e., a rubric of problems that can be posed and conceptually solved," it should in fact be conceived of as *antagonism*, or "an irreconcilable struggle between entities, or positions, the resolution of which is not dialectical but entails the obliteration of one of the positions."[6] He argues that blackness's "grammar of suffering" is not exploitation or alienation, as might be supposed under a rubric of conflict, but accumulation and fungibility, or the state of being antihuman—"a position against which Humanity establishes, maintains, and renews its coherence."[7] In other words, black lives matter only to the extent that they help establish the boundaries of what life is and what it is not. The woman at the gate is among those who understand this positionality most instinctively, for hers is an "ethical grammar" that calls to question not simply the actions of the world but the world itself.[8] Of course she must be crazy. By leveling her critique physically and symbolically at the purported threshold of intellectual life and progress and forcing an encounter that, whether avoided or disavowed, had to be *dealt with*, she occasioned a reckoning with blackness, however brief, that refused the mandates of both intellectual and social protocols. This is to say, what it meant for the crazy woman to be crazy was to assert a claim against the very enabling conditions of her craziness.

For black women craziness and anger very often go hand in hand. Claudia Rankine demonstrates this correspondence masterfully in her discussion of Serena Williams's epic takedown of a lineswoman at the 2009 US Open. In contrast to the "commodified" anger Jayson Musson–as–Hennessy Youngman advocates in his parodic online tutorial "How to Be a Successful Black Artist," wherein he provides advice on how to purposefully cultivate an "angry nigger exterior," Rankine is concerned with addressing a more daily and ordinary "actual anger," the expression of which "might make the witness believe that a person is 'insane.'"[9] She argues that Williams's response to a questionable-at-best foot-fault call, during which she walked toward the offending lineswoman and told her, "I swear to God I'll take this fucking ball and shove it down your fucking throat, you hear me? I swear to God!" was not about *that* moment but about the whole series of moments that occasioned it, not the least of which was a similarly egregious string of calls made by the chair umpire Mariana Alves at the US Open five years earlier. But lest we think Williams's anger a minor thing having only to do with the discrepancies of specific individuals, when Rankine claims that Williams was "fighting crazily against the so-called wrongness of her body's positioning at the service line,"[10] she reminds us that Williams's most serious violations of tennis etiquette have nothing to do with her actions on the court but the fact that she is there at all and that because not only is she there but she is the *best* there, she, like the crazy woman railing at the gate, forces an irreconcilable reckoning. Her anger is thus a "type of knowledge" that "responds to insult and attempted erasure simply by asserting *presence*."[11] And after the inevitable aftermath, after the delayed apology and the hefty fine and the prolonged probation, a "newly contained,"[12] that is, a more calm and measured and *civilized* Williams claimed it was one of her various alters, Tequanda, the unchristian girl from the hood, who showed up/out at the US Open in 2009.[13] What we might gather from Williams, then, is that she is indeed crazy or, more precisely, that craziness is the condition of containing black female anger.[14]

Anger is etymologically derived from the Old Norse term *angr*, which means "distress," "suffering," or "anguish," and the Proto-Indo-European root *angh*, meaning "tight, painfully constricted, painful."[15] If, as Wilderson suggests, the grammar of black suffering is an unspoken antagonism, then I want to posit anger as an exposure or an *embodiment* of what Stefano Harney and Fred Moten refer to as "the sense of dispossession and possession by the dispossessed," or "the general antagonism."[16] In other words anger is not simply the assertion of presence *but presence itself*. It is a critical posture toward suffering and constraint that is irreducible to suffering and disruptive of constraint—a "riotous production of difference."[17] And if the general antagonism is a *collective* sense or "a kind of way of being with others,"[18] then anger is, similarly, a way of being that cannot *be* in isolation. Put another way, the crazy woman yelling at the gate is only crazy insofar as there is something against which to mark off her craziness, and what she and Serena Williams–cum–Tequanda enact cannot be summed up as complaint against either the white folks or their position within the structure of antagonisms but is instead the disruption of positionality by way of the refusal to "issue the call to order"[19] and the attendant extension and preservation of a mode of affective sociality essential to black social life.

A RIOTOUS PRODUCTION OF DIFFERENCE

Toni Morrison knew before she even started writing her second novel, *Sula*, first published in 1973, that it would conclude, "girl, girl, girlgirlgirl."[20] In its final form this ending is the opening onto a bottomless cry, a belated dirge for a forsaken friendship and a death that inaugurated an immeasurable loss. That "girl" was to be the final word and that this word was revealed to Morrison first suggests its significance not only to the text itself but also to the experience that helped occasion the text, which in this case was time spent in the company of single and separated black mothers living in Queens, New York, in the late 1960s, whose relative isolation and dire economic circumstances afforded them the opportunity to rely on and befriend each other and the space to think creatively. This period of what she refers to as "escape from male rule"[21] enabled Morrison to write the novel that, of her oeuvre, most intimately attends to the life-world of black women.

Perhaps nothing is more illustrative of this attentiveness than the invocation of "girl"—an important and unparalleled term in the black female lexicon—throughout the text. Sometimes "girl" means just what it means, of course, but the terms by which black women take it up often belie its most basic dictionary definition.[22] While there are any number of different instances in which "girl" might be invoked by black females across the age spectrum, at its most substantive it is an expression of claim and affection among black girls and women. This is no minor thing, particularly given the term's racist history as it relates to black women. Before we ever get to "girl" in *Sula*, its etymological stakes are made apparent. The story that centers the novel begins in 1920 with a ten-year-old Nel Wright, the eventual best, and only, friend of the eponymous protagonist, on her first and only trip outside the Bottom, a black enclave set way up in the hills of the fictional town of Medallion, Ohio, with her mother, Helene. Helene has structured her life and, consequently, Nel's life in direct opposition to the life she knew growing up the daughter of a Creole whore, and it is not until the impending death of the grandmother who raised her that she ventures back to the home in New Orleans she has worked so diligently to escape the vestiges of by way of her proper comportment and staunch respectability—she is a member of the most conservative church in town (because there is no Catholic church), is fastidious in her adherence to social protocols and demands the same of others, commands significant authority in the community, and is "very particular about her friends" (22). The journey has only just begun when Helene inadvertently enters the wrong car of the train she and Nel are to travel down south on (that is, the one not marked "colored only"), and she is subsequently confronted by a white train conductor, who says to her, "What you think you doin', gal?" (20).

> So soon. So soon. She hadn't even begun the trip back. Back to her grandmother's house in the city where the red shutters glowed, and already she had been called, "gal." All the old vulnerabilities, all the old fears of being somehow flawed gathered in her stomach and made her hands tremble. She had heard only that one word; it dangled above her wide-brimmed hat, which had slipped, in her exertion, from its carefully leveled placement and was now tilted in a bit of a jaunt over her eye. (20)

The physical and emotional effect of the train conductor's comment on Helene reveals the extent to which, not unlike the use of *boy* in reference to black men, *gal* gets used in the service of reinforcing the subservient positionality of black women. Helene is so disconcerted by the train conductor's treatment of her (and that this is an *uncommon* experience for Helene is revealing) that her instinctive response is to pardon herself and smile "dazzlingly and coquettishly" (21) at the train conductor. The other black passengers in attendance, particularly two male soldiers, are obviously deeply upset at Helene's seeming inability or unwillingness to resist, even tacitly, the conductor's offense, and Nel looks on as the men's eyes begin "bubbling with a hatred for her mother that had not been there in the beginning but had been born with the dazzling smile" (22). Candice Jenkins argues that the offending smile should not be read as Helene's acquiescence to the train conductor's insult, however, but as an act "meant to distinguish her from the other blacks in the car, to make the conductor see her as exemplary—thereby lessening her vulnerability in the face of his power. In other words, that smile is not an *acceptance* of Helene's own lower caste position with respect to the conductor, but is her attempted *resistance* to that position."[23] Jenkins goes on to argue that Helene's attempt at resistance ultimately fails because rather than distinguishing her from those "other" black people, including her own whore of a mother, it merely reinforces the narrative of sexual availability ascribed to black women that her stringent propriety is otherwise meant to repudiate.[24]

Given this moment as context, I want to suggest that *Sula* is in rebellion against precisely the narrative it produces—not only the racism represented by the train conductor but also the codification of racism represented by Helene's corresponding performance of moral rectitude and questionable resistance. The reclamation of "gal" to "girl" later in the text discretely signals this rebellion, but it is Sula Peace who, by reclaiming her *self*, most actively embodies it. Indeed Hortense Spillers refers to Morrison's text as "the single most important irruption of black women's writing in our era" and to Sula as "a kind of countermythology" whose "outlawry may not be the best kind, but that she has the will toward rebellion itself *is* the stunning idea."[25] Nel's cry at the end of the text that she, whose "parents had succeeded in rubbing down to a dull glow any sparkle or splutter she had" (83), and Sula, whose "experimental life" marked her as evil among her fellow townspeople (118), were "girls together" (174) is not just a lament for her dead friend but an insight into the latent commutability of Sula's outlawry. Put differently, Nel's own "will toward rebellion" was both concealed by and embodied within Sula, the presumed antithesis of her own godly respectability.[26] Sula's allegedly "feeble-minded" (171) grandmother Eva Peace, whom Sula controversially had committed to a home for the elderly upon her return to the Bottom following a ten-year absence, makes this mutuality explicit when, after Sula's death, she tells Nel that she and Sula were "Just alike. Both of you. Never was no difference between you" (169).

In an interview conducted with Morrison in 1981 during which she discussed the similarities between her hometown of Lorain, Ohio, and the black community characterized in *Sula*, the author opined,

It seems to me there were more excesses in women and men, and people accepted them as they don't now. In the black community where I grew up, there was eccentricity and freedom, less conformity in individual habits—but close conformity in terms of the survival of the village, of the tribe. Before sociological microscopes were put on us, people did anything and nobody was run out of town. I mean, the community in *Sula* let her stay. They wouldn't wash or bury her. They protected themselves from her, but she was part of the community. The detritus of white people, the rejects from the respectable white world, which appears in *Sula* was in our neighborhood. In my family there were some really interesting people who were willing to be whatever they were. People permitted it, perhaps because in the outer world the eccentrics had to be a little servant person or a low-level factory worker. They had an enormous span of emotions and activities, and they are the people I remember when I go to write. When I go to colleges, the students say "Who are these people?" Maybe it's because now everybody seems to be trying to be "right."[27]

Sula is the most ready embodiment of eccentricity in the Bottom; and not only is she *not* run out of town, but she is responded to, like all "oppressive oddities," with "an acceptance that borders on welcome" (89). Although she does nothing that on the face of it is as vicious as what her grandmother Eva does to Plum, her drug-addicted son whom she sets on fire in order to prevent from "crawling back in her womb" (71), and despite the fact that her sexual liaisons with married men are seemingly no more frequent than those her mother Hannah engaged in before her own fiery death, Sula becomes the structuring force of evil in the Bottom. So significant is her presence that after her death to an unnamed illness the community itself begins to disintegrate.

The tension was gone and so was the effort they made. Without her mockery, affection for others sank into flaccid disrepair. Daughters who had complained bitterly about the responsibilities of taking care of their aged mothers-in-law had altered when Sula locked Eva away, and they began cleaning those old women's spittoons without a murmur. Now that Sula was dead and done with, they returned to a steeping resentment of the burdens of old people. Wives uncoddled their husbands; there seemed no further need to reinforce their variety. And even those

Negroes who had moved down from Canada to Medallion, who re-
marked every chance they got that they had never been slaves, felt a
loosening of the reactionary compassion for Southern-born blacks Sula
had inspired in them. They returned to their original claims of superiority. (153–54)

Sula's original sin is thus not about anything she does but about who she is
and what she represents. She rejects the "sociomoral constructs"[28] that tra-
ditionally conscript the lives of women into the roles of wife and mother or
their semblances and "lives out her days exploring her own thoughts and
emotions, giving them full reign, feeling no obligation to please anybody
unless their pleasure pleased her" (118). Even the most heinous behavior of
her grandmother and mother, whose lives are integral in defining Sula's life,
ultimately correspond to the mother/wife roles—Eva's assault on Plum is
her attempt at saving him from himself, and Hannah's affairs were a "com-
pliment" to the wives whose husbands she treated with kindness and generosity (115). By comparison, when Sula's mother catches fire and begins
burning to death, Sula merely watches with interest (75), and her practice
of trying out once and then discarding the local husbands without any dis-
cernible excuse is deemed an unparalleled offense (115). By devoting herself
to her own self-making, even to the point of owning her own loneliness
(143), Sula acknowledges "no framework of moral reference beyond or other
than herself."[29]

Sula is, in essence, the very articulation of black female anger. To be
clear, I am not suggesting a correspondence of behavior but of posture.
More precisely, Sula's posture is disruptive of positionality, or the state of
being positioned. To return to a term introduced earlier, she is the antagonism that makes the entire structure cohere. Although her actual physical
threat is minimal at best, her sense of herself, her desire to attend to her own
self-interests and to "exist foremost in her own consciousness,"[30] threatens
to upend the entire system (what kind of devastation would have been
wrought, for instance, if Nel and the other women of the Bottom had taken
Sula's lead?), and so the system must continuously and actively align itself
against not just her body but her very way of being. Thus what it is to claim
anger as critical posture is to assert a presence that wills to self-possession.
It is the disruption of constraint, a riotous force of differentiation and remaking in a world structured by regularity.

CODA

My Aunt Sweet, who lived for a time with my biological parents before they divorced, likes to tell a certain story of me as a young child around the age of three. As the story goes, when my mother would be preoccupied with other matters, say, cooking, and my father would be who knows where, I was in the habit of grabbing my little dog (I think his name was Fluffy) by the ear and dragging him along behind me as I walked in circles around the house moaning, "uuunh, uuunh." I wouldn't be crying exactly, just audibly registering an indefinable and ceaseless complaint to the extreme irritation of my aunt and the seeming indifference of my mother—which might explain why my mother has no recollection of this ever having happened and my aunt remembers, and tells it, like it was yesterday. There exists a school picture that was taken of me around this same general time period, and in it I sit in a green dress and white tights, my hair pulled up into crisscrossing braids on top of my head and a *Tweety & Sylvester* book on my lap as I look into the camera, my lips set into an unrepentant pout. In later school pictures, which my mother mandated I pose for every year, I at least pretended to smile. But in the picture with the green dress I was too young to care much about pleasing anyone, and I still get a bit of a perverse kick out of thinking about the photographer contorting their face and flailing about trying to get me to crack even the smallest of smiles for the sake of the picture, all to no avail.

My aunt's irritation aside, at the age of three my willfulness might, I imagine, have been considered cute, easy to manage or dismiss as typical preadolescent (mis)behavior. But as I got older and my childhood temper tantrums and pouts gave way to what eventually came to be known as my "attitude problem," the stakes had obviously become much higher—as most of the disciplinary measures used against me had to do with my "smart mouth" and the unfortunate habit my eyes had of rolling around in their sockets. While I had a tendency toward becoming the teacher's pet, if, for whatever reason, I didn't like a teacher, they were typically made aware of it (by me)—and if things got too out of hand, so too were my parents (by the teacher). Besides adult types, my attitude even worked on the nerves of some of my friends, to the point where my best friend (temporarily) called off our friendship in grade school. Still, my problem was not as much disciplinary as it had to do with my general disposition. Despite the trouble my mouthiness sometimes got me into, I was rather rule abiding—I was never given to physical altercations; I skipped much of the typical teenage acting-out behavior, including sneaking out and sneaking folks in (well, with the exception of a couple of *minor* incidents), and consequently never had an official curfew; and I was quite clear about where my parents drew the line on the decibel level and tone of my voice, no matter how mad I might want to call myself. My anger, contained as it was, was my primary rebellion.

As I got older, I came to understand that this condition I was afflicted with was endemic to black women and that it had a particular resonance in relationship to black men, especially given that I, like almost every other black woman I knew before I left home for college, was raised under the mandate of a Christian ethic that requires women to dutifully submit to their husbands and the other male authority figures in their lives. Angry black women like me, it was said, who were willing to openly, and sometimes quite forcefully, contradict our male counterparts, along with our general unwillingness to smile on command or otherwise cater to their overtures, however jacked up they might be, were running good black men away and making ourselves much less viable as marital companions. Of course, this notion of the angry black woman is ultimately but a variation on a common and enduring theme that black women are ruining the family structure and otherwise undermining the development of the larger black community.

But despite the agony I was sometimes in over what seemed like an assault on my very way of being, I eventually began to recognize in these other women called angry—or crazy or bitter or mean or (too) serious or simply *off*—something of myself that I willed toward. First and foremost was my mother, who, although she is the single most loving and sincerely *righteous* person I have ever known, has never lost the "don't start nothin'" spark that she bequeathed to her daughter and that her mother bequeathed to her. And there was my seventh-grade English teacher, Ms. Birditt, whom my classmates and I were sure was all the way out of her mind and who, following a presentation I gave in Peoria a few years back, greeted me with wet eyes and a smothering hug. It turns out we were right. Ms. Birditt was indeed crazy. For she had always been wholly, defiantly convinced about the potential of her students, regardless of what anyone else said or thought about us, and she was determined to convince *us* if she convinced no one else. Later there were other teachers, professors actually, who stood in front of the room and felt no compunction to befriend their students but simply got on with the thing they were there to do and did it well (and, in so doing, inspired others of us to do the same). There was Barb, who lived next door to me when I lived in Inglewood and kept the entire neighborhood on high alert with her (often drunken) antics but who always had a tight embrace for me when she saw me and would greet my open doorway with a "Hey, Terri" when she didn't. And there was Mrs. Sandra, my home away from home during my time in graduate school who would move heaven and earth expeditiously to help a person in need but who would also cut you if you fooled around and crossed her the wrong way. And not to be forgotten was my cousin Rosalind, who while I was in college gave me two hundred dollars I suspected she couldn't really afford to let go of so that I could buy my books for the coming semester. When I inevitably started sobbing that I didn't know when I would be able to pay her back, she told me, as is her way, to "shut up 'cause ain't nobody said you had to pay anything back" and never spoke another word about it.

There are so many others—so many black women who have, at one time or another, been defined by their anger. The point here is not to suggest that our anger is always to the good but to query what we might lose if we fail to acknowledge the significance of anger as something more than an errant emotion that must be disavowed or displaced in order for black women to be legible as something other than who we are. In a context in which we have been bought, sold, and possessed many times over, black women's will to self-possession is the ultimate rebellion. It is, as Audre Lorde has taught us, *survival*.[31] Perhaps, as my erstwhile friend suggested, I really am too close to anger. But at least I'm in good company.

2

GETTING HAPPY

There is no music like that music, no drama like the drama of the saints rejoicing, the sinners moaning, the tambourines racing, and all those voices coming together and crying holy unto the Lord. There is still, for me, no pathos quite like the pathos of those multicolored, worn, somehow triumphant and transfigured faces, speaking from the depths of a visible, tangible, continuing despair of the goodness of the Lord. I have never seen anything to equal the fire and excitement that sometimes, without warning, fill a church, causing the church, as Leadbelly and so many others have testified, to "rock." Nothing that has happened to me since equals the power and the glory that I sometimes felt when, in the middle of a sermon, I knew that I was somehow, by some miracle, really carrying, as they said, "the Word"—when the church and I were one. Their pain and their joy were mine, and mine were theirs—they surrendered their joy and pain to me, I surrendered mine to them—and their cries of "Amen!" and "Hallelujah!" and "Yes, Lord!" and "Praise His name!" and "Preach it, brother!" sustained and whipped on my solos until we all became equal, wringing wet, singing and dancing, in anguish and rejoicing, at the foot of the alter.

—JAMES BALDWIN, *THE FIRE NEXT TIME*

Growing up, I was primarily raised in Baptist churches. My mother, grandmother, and that entire side of the family, so far as I knew, were Baptists. So was my stepdad and most of his family. My biological father would refer to himself as Pentecostal if you asked him. But given that I had never known him to set foot inside a church unless it was for a funeral or a wedding or, at my request, the occasional choir concert (although, as the story goes, at one point in time he was quite the Christian soldier), my dad's supposed Pentecostalism didn't much concern me. It wasn't until I was in fifth grade and became best friends with a girl who lived a few blocks down the street from me, whose entire upbringing had been Pentecostal, specifically COGIC, that I began to gather that there was something different, at least superficially, between our faith traditions. (Testament to the particular demographics of Peoria, we eventually learned that both my dad and my friend's mother had migrated from the same community in West Memphis, Arkansas. It turned out that they and many of their siblings had attended the same high school.) Both my friend and I were consummate church girls, raised to believe wholeheartedly in the tenets of Christianity and to understand that church was not just a once-a-week pastime but the bedrock of our very existence, and we were both preacher's kids—my stepdad accepted "the call" to ministry during my youth, and her father was the pastor of the church her family attended. We were both indoctrinated into what it meant to be good Christian girls who would evolve into virtuous Christian women: we must keep our bodies and our homes neat and clean at all times (we both gave our parents absolute fits due to our messy bedrooms; I, at least, have since been redeemed); we must be respectful of all authority figures and obey the rules they handed down (in this case the only real trouble I ever got into had to do with my persistent "attitude problem," while my friend was, shall we say, a bit more adventurous in her troublemaking); we must remain strong in our spiritual walks, taking dedicated time out for God every day (which we did with varying degrees of success, depending on what else we had going on); and we must absolutely, positively, beyond a shadow of a doubt, ceaselessly, prayerfully, and with all our youthful vigor, *keep our legs closed*—to men indefinitely and to women eternally.

So it was with my best friend, tucked away in a corner of our South Side neighborhood at her father's tiny church, that I had my first personal experience with the Holy Ghost. Now, despite what some of your Pentecostal friends might tell you, Baptists do actually know a thing or two about the Holy Ghost. I had often seen folks shouting and jumping and running and whooping and hollering in the churches my family belonged to. I had known them to speak in tongues and prophesy and participate in the laying on of hands—all of that. But it wasn't until I attended one of my friend's midweek services that I began to get an inkling that "catching the

Holy Ghost," or what the saints also call "getting happy," was, for some Christians, of fundamental importance. I believe I was probably an adult before I understood just how important the indwelling of the Spirit, and the evidence of that indwelling, is to Pentecostalism, but as a grade-school outsider at my friend's Holy Ghost–filled church, all I could really comprehend was that there seemed to be a marked sense of urgency to *their* shouting and dancing and laying on of hands. And so there was. In a church that had no more than fifteen pews and just a few handfuls of members, I couldn't hide my twelve- or thirteen-year-old self that day. The praises were going up, the blessings were (hopefully) coming down, the Spirit was high, and my best friend had abandoned me—she was off somewhere playing the drums (my girl is an awesome percussionist) or banging on a tambourine or jumping up and down on a wall or something—when they came for me. Much of the memory is hazy, but what I do clearly remember is suddenly being surrounded by women beseeching me to "let go," "give in," and "let God have His way." It was apparent they wanted something not just from me but *for* me.

I am tempted to front and say that it is only because of my training as a rule-abiding good girl that I "gave in," that it was all a bit of a put-on for the sake of the imposing church women who were so desperately crowding around me, but that wouldn't be quite truthful. What is more true is that one minute I was minding my own business, sightseeing and clapping along neatly as the organ thundered and the shouting music raged on, and the next thing I knew *I* was the one jumping up and down, shouting and crying—getting happy. It felt like I'd had a momentary blackout, because it wasn't clear how I'd transitioned from one stage to the other, how I, who has never had much of an affinity for losing control of anything, anywhere, at any time, ever, was so abruptly taken over by something that was outside of myself, or inside of myself, as the case may be. In any event, when I came to, I knew that I had experienced something altogether different than I'd experienced in all of my previous churchgoing years (or that I have experienced since). Had I asked the congregants of my friend's church, they would probably have told me that what they wanted so deeply for me was *salvation*, which, I suppose, would have been most radically manifested by my speaking in tongues, at which I ultimately fell short, although according to my own tradition I had been "saved" since uttering the prayer of salvation in front of my home congregation some years prior.

The point is, in spite of the doctrinal differences between our respective denominations, throughout our childhoods, our teenage years, and into our adulthoods, my friend and I continued to be shaped not just by the faith traditions we had been individually born into but also by each other's experiences of those traditions. While the strictures placed on my friend were in some ways more severe than those placed on me—for many years she was forbidden to wear pants or makeup, and even things like playing games involving dice or going to the movie theater were off-limits for a time—we both knew the confines of Christian religiosity intimately. For my part, I was always particularly resistant to the restriction against secular music. Many were the days I sat crouched in front of the little television in my basement bedroom watching music videos on BET and MTV (back in the days before YouTube created videos on demand and you had to actually keep your station of choice on lock if you hoped to catch your jam of the moment), the volume turned down low, my hand resting inches from the knob just in case a parent unexpectedly came to the door and I needed to quickly turn the channel. For years as an adult I struggled terribly with the effects of the churchgirlism that caused me to have to play catch-up with some of the more significant moments in 1990s popular music history that I missed in between channel flips.

The agony over my restricted music catalogue aside, there was probably nothing my friend and I struggled with more than the all-important abstinence mandate. While her father was a bit looser in this area, telling her that while he wanted her to remain abstinent, he understood the temptations of the flesh and cautioned her safety, my stepdad's way was to scare me into submission. I specifically remember him summoning me to the kitchen table, where all of the serious family conversations usually took place, and being warned against premarital sex with the ominous prediction that if I did not wait until I was married, I would undoubtedly get pregnant the very first time I had sex because "I knew better." (In his defense, the youngest of my stepdad's three older daughters had been, like me, a bookish honor roll student growing up and because she had gotten pregnant while in high school, he always seemed to have a lingering fear that I would somehow end up sharing her fate.) Still, my parents had always made it very clear that they would never, under any condition, abandon me, that even if I did something as "foolish" as to get pregnant while still a teenager they would continue to love and support me. And so it was at least partially because of their unwavering support and the consistently high expectations my parents always had of me that I went through an abstinence program and publicly took the abstinence pledge at my church while I was in high school. For if there was anything I feared more than my parents' anger, it was their disappointment.

It is against this sort of background, one that is my own but that I would venture to say a significant percentage of black women have at least a passing familiarity with, that I want to consider the relay between what Baldwin refers to in *The Fire Next Time* as the "pathos" of the black church[1] and the church girls-turned-matrons he references earlier in that same text. While speaking about the severe religious transformation he underwent at the age of fourteen, Baldwin notes his acute awareness of the changes that were also apparent in the "holy girls" who surrounded him at the time:

> In the case of the girls, one watched them turning into matrons before they had become women. They began to manifest a curious and really rather terrifying single-mindedness. It is hard to say exactly how this was conveyed: something implacable in the set of the lips, something farseeing (seeing what?) in the eyes, some new and crushing determination in the walk, something peremptory in the voice. They did not tease us, the boys, any more; they reprimanded us sharply, saying "You better be thinking about your soul!" For the girls saw the evidence on the Avenue, knew what the price would be, for them, of one misstep, knew that they had to be protected and that we were the only protection there was. They understood that they must act as God's decoys, saving the souls of the boys for Jesus and binding the bodies of the boys in marriage.[2]

Ten years earlier, in his autobiographical first novel, *Go Tell It on the Mountain*, Baldwin had used the four women central to its narrative, Elizabeth, Florence, Deborah, and Esther, to elaborate on the condition of "God's decoys." Whether they represent the epitome of Christian womanhood (Elizabeth and Deborah) or are the prototypes of fallen female virtue (Florence and Esther), Baldwin's women are boxed in by the church, hemmed in by the mandates of a strict black charismatic tradition that assigns them to particular roles from which they must not depart (dutiful mother, all-suffering wife, faithful witness, chaste servant) lest they be consigned to the realm of the wicked, a place where there is neither reprieve from, nor remedy for, the disreputable harlot. Even Elizabeth and Deborah, God's holy vessels, were once fallen women—Deborah because she was raped by a group of white men when she was just sixteen and Elizabeth because she bore her oldest son, John, the story's protagonist and Baldwin's correlate, out of wedlock—who were only redeemed from their dishonor by way of marrying Gabriel, whose own sins are carefully safeguarded by all four women.

Despite the unbridled oppressions of this regime delineated by Baldwin, I am interested in two specific, albeit fleeting, moments in the text that register Baldwin's own conflicted relationship to the church and are, I submit, the opening onto a more expansive view of black women's complex relationship with the church and Christianity more generally. The first of these moments comes when Florence, Gabriel's prodigal sister who has avoided the church for the better part of her life, kneels at the altar of the Temple of the Fire Baptized in search of an elusive healing for an illness that is threatening her life. There she begins singing "Standing in the Need of Prayer," a song, the only song she can remember, that was her mother's, and "kneeling as she had not knelt for many years, and in this company before the altar, she gained again from the song the meaning it had held for her mother, and gained a new meaning for herself."[3] The second moment comes at the very end of the text when John is talking to Elisha, the seventeen-year-old musician and minister whom John finds himself deeply drawn to, about his religious conversion, and Elisha's laughter causes John to "observe with some wonder that a saint of God could laugh."[4]

Taken together, these moments give utterance to something I could only wonder at as a grade-schooler caught up in the religious fervor of my best friend's church. When Florence is compelled to the altar not by her own faith, which has long since evaporated, but by the faith of her long-dead mother, with whom she had a complicated and not always loving relationship, and then is able to find something for herself there, she is attesting to this thing. And when John comes to the surprising revelation that God's people do laugh, he is attesting to it too. Baldwin himself attests to it when, even long after he has taken his leave from the church, he acknowledges the unrivaled majesty of the saints in the throes of the Spirit. What they collectively confirm, in essence, is that you don't have to believe in prayer to know that it works. In other words, black religiosity far surpasses doctrine or individual beliefs or behaviors, and it resonates far beyond the confines of the church itself. Relatedly, the experience of getting happy is not contingent upon religious affiliation or adherence to particular ideological regimes.

In what follows I consider both the conditions of possibility and the socioreligious consequences of those whom Baldwin names "God's decoys" and whom I interchangeably refer to as virtuous Christian women. My concern is with thinking about what the strictures placed on black churchwomen enable discursively and materially and how these same women go about negotiating these constraints in ways that simultaneously affirm their legitimacy and challenge their authority. At the same time I want to be careful to attend to the otherworldly capacity for life yielded by the faith that Baldwin and his interlocutors attest to, which, although it perhaps surpasses all understanding, if taken seriously can help us contemplate what black churchwomen find for themselves and how it is they can get happy in conditions that might seem to predict otherwise.

THE LEXI SHOW

> My conclusion is that I'm waiting to see what God wants to do because I
> don't know who he's allowing me to experience this walk of life to minister to later on. The church has completely faggotized everybody who's
> gay, sends them to hell over the pulpit and the church literally screams
> hooray, and are happy about that. And yet we celebrate the pastor who
> has the clean record and the clean look but yet he's still doing the same
> thing that the same-gender-loving people are doing but yet he has the
> look. And so I feel that that's a community that has kept gospel alive.
> They're within the gospel community. They are human beings. And I
> believe that God loves everybody. And I believe that there are Holy
> Ghost–filled, fire-baptized, gay people.[5]

In September 2009 the artist formerly known as Tonéx caused a holy brouhaha when he effectively outed himself on *The Lexi Show*, a now-defunct Christian talk show that was hosted by gospel-singer-turned-journalist Lexi Allen on The Word Network, a Christian television network based in suburban Detroit. In the one-on-one interview Tonéx, who has since renamed and rebranded himself as indie artist B. Slade, responded to ongoing speculation about his sexuality in the affirmative, admitting that, yes, he had "experienced gay sex before" and did "lean more towards the same sex." Though he had always been controversial, Tonéx had also by that time become a very successful mainstream gospel music artist, winning or being nominated for numerous industry awards, appearing on concert billings and recording with established gospel acts such as Kirk Franklin and Trin-i-tee 5:7, and signing to major gospel music labels on which he released critically acclaimed albums. Yet ever since first coming to national attention with the release of his inaugural major-label album, *Pronounced Toe-Nay*, in 2000, the San Diego native had dodged, dismissed, and sometimes forcefully renounced accusations that he was gay or bisexual. Though such accusations are not uncommon in an industry that is relentlessly committed to the proliferation of a certain brand of hypermasculinity, in the case of Tonéx, who was frequently referred to as gospel music's version of Prince, the allegations could hardly be dismissed as mere occupational hazard. Both on stage and off his theatrics did more to inflame his critics than to quiet them. He quickly became as known for his extravagant costuming, which included top hats, feather boas, wigs, platform shoes, elaborate head wraps à la Erykah Badu, multicolored hairpieces, mohawks, and prominent piercings and tattoos, as he was for his genre-defying music. His penchant for yodeling and unabashed exhibition of his multioctave range, including a particularly strong falsetto, added an additional flare to his often highly choreographed, highly produced, stage and video performances, and his musical oeuvre was admittedly as influenced by gospel music heavyweights such as Fred Hammond and The Clark Sisters as it was by pop icons such as Prince and Michael Jackson.

The accusations regarding Tonéx's sexuality are thus part of what is at issue when during the interview Lexi begins to question him about lyrics referencing sexual molestation in "The Naked Truth," an angry, profanity-laden song he first released online in 2007. Tonéx admits to Lexi that while, yes, he had been molested as a child, he does not blame that abuse for his later "sexual explorations," including those with other men. This is a direct challenge to claims made by other Christians, gospel artist Donnie Mc-Clurkin chief among them, who claim their same-sex liaisons were the consequence of sexual abuse they suffered earlier in their lives, which then allows them to claim they have been "delivered" from homosexuality because God has "delivered" them from the psychological trauma of the sexual abuse, thereby extending the Christian notion that it is somehow possible to "pray the gay away" and that homosexuality is either an assumed or traumatically coerced "lifestyle." Following this revelation, Tonéx, ever the performer, coyly dodges Lexi's more pointed, if inartful, questions about his sexuality.

LEXI: Is . . . being attracted to men under control?
TONÉX: Under control?
LEXI: You said you were attracted to men at one point.
TONÉX: Am.
LEXI: Am?
TONÉX: Mm-hmm.
LEXI: So . . . do you practice?
TONÉX: Like piano? [*He laughs.*]
LEXI: Homosexuality. I don't know how to put that. I'm trying to put it as—I'm literally trying to put this the best—do you sleep with men?
TONÉX: I don't sleep with *men*.
LEXI: You're making this real hard for me, and you know exactly where I'm going. Um, you say you don't—when I said, "Do you struggle with homosexuality?" you said no, it wasn't a struggle.
TONÉX: It's not a struggle. No.
LEXI: What are you doing, man? Who are you dating? Are you considering dating men? Are you considering dating women? Is homosexuality—*a thing of the past for you*?
TONÉX: Is homosexuality a thing of the past? I think that when someone understands who they are sexually and they know that they're a free spirit and they understand who they are as a person, it's really difficult to label that.

Just as Tonéx refuses to be labeled musically, at one point in the interview claiming he is neither a gospel artist nor a secular artist but simply "an artist," he resists having his sexuality labeled or pigeonholed by Lexi. By the time the interview ends, he has made it quite evident what he is "doing," and attempting to "put homosexuality in the past" is not it, for he insists there is space in the Kingdom of God for everyone, including someone like himself.

Given Tonéx's prominence on the gospel music scene at the time, his revelation, quite expectedly, did not go over so well with the saints. Immediately following the airing of *The Lexi Show* interview, concerts and appearances Tonéx had lined up were canceled, his friends and colleagues in the industry grew distant, and his critics took to the Internet, radio airwaves, and pulpits to advocate the need for his Divine deliverance.[6] Before long, Tonéx had closed down his once-prolific social media sites and virtually disappeared from the public spotlight. Lexi was also careful to distance herself from her interviewee. In a postinterview segment of the show just before the final credits roll she is shown sitting alone in what is ostensibly the show's control room, where she looks sedately into the camera and provides the following disclaimer: "I would like to take this time to thank my friend and brother Tonéx for a very open, honest, and candid interview. It is my belief that a man is made for a woman, and a woman is made for a man. I believe that the Bible speaks very clearly about this. However, as a journalist it is my job to tell the story. And as a Christian it is my job to love absolutely everybody, and I do that, unequivocally and unapologetically." Thus any semblance of journalistic neutrality Lexi might have seemed committed to during the interview with Tonéx is quickly disavowed as she aligns herself both theoretically and theologically with the "hate the sin, love the sinner" rhetoric that often permeates Christian teachings.

Lexi's disclaimer after the interview is essentially the explicit manifestation of her implicit positioning within the interview. Whereas Tonéx is the morally deficient backslider, she is the righteous Christian who does not affirm Tonéx but in interviewing him is responsibly fulfilling her duties as a journalist and simultaneously following the mandates of Christian law. The narrative arc she cultivates for herself suggests she is aware of and devoted to the appropriate roles for Christian women and men, that she is responsible and committed to her work, and that even when she disagrees with the men in her midst, she remains loving and embracing toward them. Lexi's professed naivety about even the *terms* of homosexuality attests to the adulterated virtue of the übermoral Christian woman, and even her grooming adds to the narrative. She is positively feminine, her nails are manicured, her makeup is flawless and understated, her long blondish-brown hair (weave) falls down to her full breasts, which are appropriately, but stylishly, covered by a denim jacket and gold necklace, and her long black dress falls to her ankles. She is thus physically attractive without being so overtly sexual as to distract or tempt any (straight) Christian man she might come into contact with or who might be watching the show.

Consequently, Lexi's posture toward Tonéx foregrounds the intense gender dynamics that undergird the notion of Christian virtue and demonstrates the conditions under which both of them have constructed their lives and are, in their respective ways, attempting to reckon with. This dynamic is perhaps most evident in the opening segment of the interview, during which Lexi and Tonéx discuss Tonéx's styling choices and religious background.

> LEXI: So people ask me all the time, you know, "What's up with this guy?" You know, you have to know that you're controversial.
> TONÉX: Uh, yeah.
> LEXI: Okay. And what I mean by that, just, let's give some specifics. I've seen you come to the Stellar Awards with the spiked hair, with, uh, earphones, you know, huge around your neck. Uh, you've been known to wear a boa.
> TONÉX: Mm-hmm.
> LEXI: You have been known to, uh, wear makeup—
> TONÉX: Mm-hmm.
> LEXI:—in a video. Uh, you have been known to—I've seen you with a lollipop ring, uh, on your hand.
> TONÉX: Yeah, the lollipop, yeah.
> LEXI: We could go on and on. Platform shoes. Uh, wigs. Uh, bobs. And nobody ever knows what vein you're gonna come in. They never know if—what is he gonna wear today? Is he gonna wear a bob today? You know, so it—that's controversial, and you have to know that. You grew up, what, PAW [Pentecostal Assemblies of the World], COGIC [Church of God in Christ]?
> TONÉX: PAW.
> LEXI: PAW. You know, I grew up COGIC.
> TONÉX: So you know.
> LEXI: And COGIC we're—ya'll was worse than us.
> TONÉX: Uh-unh.
> LEXI: Hunh. PAW was Jesus only.
> TONÉX: No, ya'll was the ones; we couldn't see past ya'll's hats.
> LEXI: Well, excuse me, PAW—the women couldn't wear hats cause they had doilies on they heads.
> TONÉX: Not at our church. That's more the Church of the Lord Jesus Christ or Apostolic Assembly. We didn't wear the doilies.
> LEXI: Oh, you didn't do that?
> TONÉX: Uh-unh.

LEXI: But still no makeup?

TONÉX: Right.

LEXI: Skirts down to your ankles, elbows covered.

TONÉX: Yes.

LEXI: Never a piece of cleavage ever?

TONÉX: No.

LEXI: Never? No. Yeah, you were pretty strict. And for you—for you to come up through that upbringing to go all the way to the opposite side of the universe with this.

TONÉX: Yeah.

LEXI: Is this guy bipolar? Is he crazy? Is he doing this on purpose? Are you doing it to make people angry and—what are you doing?

TONÉX: I guess it's just I really don't know what else to be. It's really me. Like—

LEXI: It's really you?

TONÉX: It's always been me. Um, I don't know, it's just, I think it's not fair that because I'm black that I can't do the things that, you know, white cats do.

LEXI: I don't think it's because you're black. I totally do not believe that. What I do believe is that . . . when you grow up in the black church . . . you can't do that.

TONÉX: Right.

LEXI: You know. We frown upon that. You—*come on*, you know how we do. You can't do anything outside of, you know, wearing a suit, and you can dress down these days—

TONÉX: We grow up in arrested development. You know. I thank God for those cornerstones and those statutes that we came up under because it did become an anchor. And I was talking to a good friend that I just met, and he was telling me how ships always have an anchor, but they're not meant to stay down. They're always attached to the ship, and whenever you go off to foreign places, whenever it goes too far out there, that anchor is still there and you know where to drop it. And so that's what I have. No, undeniably and unequivocally people cannot deny the Word and the anointing.

LEXI: But you knew you were pushing the envelope a *long* time ago. You knew that.

This exchange between Lexi and Tonéx alludes that women are primarily responsible for the maintenance of Christian morality. The tight control of churchwomen's bodies, in this case via their clothing and physical appearance, is indicative of a widespread theological framework that posits the female body—and, by extension, the effeminate male body—as the prevalent source of moral and social decay. The most compelling aspect of this exchange, however, is in what goes unsaid. Lexi does not seem to find it at all odd to discuss Tonéx's styling wholly in relationship to the stylings of women, and, apparently, neither does Tonéx. They take it for granted that the prohibition against makeup, and the long skirts and covered elbows and cleavage mandated for women, which they have both, to some extent, rejected, had, or should have had, a cognizable effect on Tonéx. While Lexi defines Tonéx's style as "controversial," she never does comment directly on the topsy-turvy gender dynamics at play in Tonéx's costuming that ultimately serve to make it so controversial. In a video interview he granted blogger Darian Aaron in the weeks following his appearance on *The Lexi Show*, Tonéx contended that he was officially "a grown-ass man" as a result of his revelations. "You can't be a punk or a sissy or whatever other colloquialisms are being used and be that up front and bold and translucent, transparent, without having a—a pretty big pair of *cojones*," he insisted.[7] Tonéx's gendered (mis)performances, which are styled around the aesthetic conventions denied to the women in his denominational affiliation, are thus buttressed by his own forceful claim to a quasi-macho masculinity conceived of as courageous and truthful but simultaneously at odds with the heterosexist machismo often identified with Christian discourse.

The unspoken correlation between Tonéx's queer sartorial displays and the constrained bodily aesthetics of black churchwomen suggests the black female body both marks and *is* the boundary of normative sexual behavior and desire as it is evinced within the black church (a form of demarcation that, as we will see in chapter 4, Lindon Barrett takes up by way of the "grotesque").[8] That is to say, under the church's regulatory regime the black female body sets in oppositional relationship the moral and immoral, and becomes simultaneously the receptacle and purveyor of patriarchal desire. Under this mandate, not only is the virtuous Christian woman "God's decoy" in the sense that she must save the souls of Christian boys and men, per Baldwin, but she conditions *all* appropriate Christian behavior. When Lexi urges Tonéx to admit that he is intentionally pushing the envelope through his styling choices, telling him *"come on, you know how we do,"* she is subtly critiquing the edicts that govern, or attempt to govern, them both and simultaneously confirming her relationship to Tonéx's plight, even as she works to distance herself from it. And though she never strays too far from the moral high ground, her ability to find *common* ground signals the complex entanglement between deviance and righteousness as embodied by presumptively heterosexual women and lesbian, gay, bisexual, transgender, queer, or, as Tonéx would have it, same-gender-loving people in the black church.

Accordingly, what is most provocatively demonstrated here is that "the negative, the expended, the excessive invariably form the ground of possibilities for value," and negativity is value's "essential resource."[9] In other words, while Lexi will not, indeed cannot, affirm Tonéx, *she* is affirmed by the very fact of her denial—he is the open secret that allows her denial to adhere. Tonéx's fugitive existence, to the extent that it *is* fugitive, relies on and is fundamentally conditioned by his co-option of the female form, and it is against this very fugitivity that the virtuous Christian woman attains meaning. In short, Tonéx and Lexi confirm each other's place in the socio-religious hierarchy and consequently reveal the correspondence between "defilement and the positive structure of which it bears a concealed relation."[10]

In C. Riley Snorton's analysis of the "down low," which he uses not just as a term to identify black men who have sex with men and do not identify as gay, bisexual, or queer but as a framework for conceptualizing black sexual representation more generally, he contends that, "drawing on the pervasive stereotype of homosexual contagion and the reiterative coupling of hemophilia and homophobia, the putatively queer black figure stands in as the one we fear and blame, as the personification of black moral and sexual capability, as an irreparable failure in practicing personal responsibility."[11] By outlining the anxieties surrounding men who exhibit nonnormative forms of masculinity in the church, particularly musicians and choir directors, alongside the fallout from the scandal that broke around Bishop Eddie Long in 2010—during which the megachurch pastor was accused of sexual misconduct by four young men with whom he later settled lawsuits—Snorton posits the down-low figure as one who "threatens the black church's representational claim to moral legitimacy and authority."[12] In the current instance Lexi is both the embodiment of the "moral legitimacy and authority" that Tonéx puts at risk and the antidote to the sexual pathology he represents, not only because of her assumed heterosexuality but also because she adheres to the appropriate gender norms and behavior befitting God's decoy. She is, in effect, the "proverbial salve"[13] to Tonéx's "wounded" sexuality. But while Lexi represents a study in unsullied Christian virtue, what I take up next is a discussion of someone who unreservedly presents her *failures* as the admonishment to virtuous Christian womanhood.

NO MORE SHEETS

The abstinence pledge I took while in high school continued to be a monumental thorn in my side throughout my college years. Especially given that I was no longer under the watchful eyes of my parents and was instead living in a place—the university residence hall—that at times seemed wholly dedicated to the rampant production and even more rampant release of sexual tension, I struggled with it programmatically (*What is one actually expected to do about their hormones? Is masturbation a viable option? Can one engage in oral sex and still proudly proclaim one's virginity? Sure, true love is supposed to wait, but just how long is it expected to wait if marriage is not actually a top priority?*) but also in terms of what it meant for me as a young black woman who was desperately trying to figure myself out racially, sexually, and otherwise. And so it was during this period that I attended a "No More Sheets" party hosted by one of my friends in the Young Adult Ministry that I was a part of at my Chicago church home.

"No More Sheets" is the title of both a sermon and a book by Juanita Bynum, who rose to prominence in the late 1990s initially due to her association with Dallas-based "neo-Pentecostal" megachurch pastor T. D. Jakes, one of the most, if not *the* most, high-profile black preachers of the late twentieth and early twenty-first centuries.[14] Jakes's expansive empire was largely founded on a diverse network of ministries arranged around the leitmotif "Woman, Thou Art Loosed," which caters, in particular, to women in need of spiritual, emotional, and physical healing. What first began in 1992 as a Sunday school group-therapy session at a church he was pastoring in his hometown of Charleston, West Virginia, eventually morphed into a lucrative franchise featuring a national best-selling book and several corresponding books including a Bible, a Grammy-nominated CD, a 2004 motion picture directed by Michael Schultz, and an annual women's conference that attracts as many as eighty thousand participants each year.[15] It was to one of these early conferences, which was configured specifically for singles, that Jakes invited Bynum to preach and where she first delivered "No More Sheets" the sermon, wherein she boldly attests to being delivered by God from a sexually promiscuous past. After releasing "No More Sheets" to video and publishing the corresponding book, *No More Sheets: The Truth about Sex*, in 1998, Bynum quickly began to draw thousands of her own devoted followers. Before long she was following in the mode of Jakes, publishing best-selling books, headlining major conferences, and eventually becoming a fixture on TBN, a Christian-based television network that advertises itself as "America's most watched faith channel."[16] However, in 2007 a very public domestic-abuse scandal involving her then-husband, Thomas W. Weeks III, a pastor she had married in a televised million-dollar ceremony five years earlier, dealt a severe blow to any hopes she might have had of becoming Jakes's female counterpart.[17]

Despite Bynum's eventual public decline, she is significant for becoming one of very few black women to break into the heavily male-dominated network of televangelists and high-profile religious leaders who hold rank in black Christendom. This is due in no small part to her ability to connect with her audience by using her own life as the basis of her message, thereby exposing her vulnerabilities and, most notably, her sexual indiscretions in ways that have historically been very difficult for black women generally and black churchwomen in particular to do publicly. Theologian Renita Weems admits as much when she claims, "I wouldn't say her preaching or theology is revolutionary. But living a promiscuous life, it's not that women haven't heard that message, it's just they're not accustomed to women in ministry admitting to that in the pulpit."[18] Indeed Bynum's claim to fame and the force of her moral proselytizing inheres in the slut-to-saint narrative she deftly weaves around herself in "No More Sheets," which, for the sake of discussion, I break down here into three parts: the exposure, the exhortation, and the divination.

Part I: The Exposure

The prophetess stands in the middle of a stage where T. D. Jakes, his wife, Serita Jakes, and several other ministerial types are positioned off to the left. As the camera pans out into the vast arena, we see thousands upon thousands of people standing on their feet clapping. There is the occasional man, a white woman comes into view every now and then, but the thousands gathered here are primarily black women. After settling the audience and dispensing with the preacherly formalities, Bynum, who is dressed in a formless pink suit, its ankle-length skirt and a white scarf tied around her throat concealing any possible hint of forbidden skin, begins to talk solemnly about the "awesome task" and responsibility that has been set before her for this occasion. This God-given task requires that she exhibit "no flesh," and just as she has endeavored to conceal her literal flesh, she must conceal, or defeat, the human, fleshly limitations that would otherwise thwart her from her task. It is Divine irony. For the mandate that she exhibit no flesh ultimately demands that she reveal her fleshiest desires. And so she says she could not dare speak at a singles conference about being single "without dipping into [her] own business" because, as God put it to her, "How can you help somebody if you don't tell anybody where you've been?" Accordingly, Bynum reveals that "where she's been" is single, raised in the Church of God in Christ to remain a virgin until she was married, which she did, but since getting married and then divorced has had to experience singleness differently, as a woman who understands the pleasures of sex firsthand. What this has consequently occasioned is a fierce spiritual battle:

> Even today I'm struggling with a couple of things right now. You don't want me to tell the truth, right? You want me to stand up here and act like because I got this mic in my hand that I'm just so sold out for Jesus that don't nothin' bother me! I'm just all in the anointing! And I don't never get frustrated! I don't never wanna fall and have some sex! I don't never wanna do nothin' wrong! But the devil is a liar! Come on here somebody! Every day of my life, *I'm struggling, to kill, the flesh!* . . .
>
> You know what, ya'll can beg to differ to me if you want to, but I find it very difficult to listen to anybody preach to me about being single when they got a pair of thighs in they bed every night! You know, when you rollin' over in the sheets and you keep telling me to "Hold on, honey, sanctify yourself!" and you goin' home to biceps and triceps and big old muscles and thighs; you got somebody giving you back rubs! No, no, no, you go sit down! I want to hear "hold on" from somebody who is really holding on! I want to hear "hold on" from somebody that *knows* my struggle![19]

By this time the place is thundering. As far as the eye can see women, and the occasional man, are on their feet shouting out their "amens" and "go 'heads." And ahead she goes. Bynum contends that she's been to all the singles conferences and taken all of the religious advice and tried all of the righteous remedies, including buying herself flowers and pretty pajamas and pampering herself, and "it didn't satisfy nothin'." Then she claims there are those people "that's not really saved and consecrated" who have suggested masturbation to her, but she's not trying to be in the situation in which she has to go to the altar and repent because she "took care of herself." If she has to go to the altar anyway, she's going to go because she "had it all night and all day." That shouts 'em.

Part II: The Exhortation

Now they are ready. Bynum has formulated her entire opening monologue around the question that presumably motivates the majority of the women in the room and is, apparently, the only viable solution to their collective struggles in the flesh. That is, "Why am I not married?" The answer: because "you're not single yet." Here again she uses her own story as leverage for the lesson she wants to impart. She contends that every time she had sex with a man she was engaging in an act of "consummation" and was effectively marrying him. Thus when she went to God with her frustrations about being single, He told her she could not get married yet because she had already been married too many times. Further, there is a "penalty" to be paid for every person slept with outside of marriage, and the spirit of each person the unwed person has sex with stays with her until she is "processed" by God and thereby "purged" of those spirits. Bynum's point, then, is that the problem with single women is not the men but the women themselves. They are not married because they have not dealt with the spirits from their pasts that are holding them in bondage. What's more, not only are they spiritually unprepared for marriage, but like she herself once was, they are emotionally, financially, and domestically unprepared as well:

> I wanna get married and you can't even cook! I wanna get married and your nails too long to make a biscuit! I wanna get married and you can't even wash clothes! I wanna get married and you here at the conference and your bedroom at home is tore up, and your house is nasty! Aw, ya'll

ain't sayin' nothin'! You in debt and can't pay your bills, every dime you get is on your back right *now*, Ms. I Wanna Get Married!

"I love you" don't keep the gas on! "I love you" don't keep the bills paid! See, let me help ya'll with something. I wanna tell ya'll this right now. And I'm just gonna tell you the truth. We always talkin' 'bout, "all our black brothers is goin' out and gettin' all these white ladies. What's wrong? We ain't good enough?" Naw, we too needy. We ain't got nothin'. Come on, ya'll ain't sayin' nothin'. I'm supposed to be a helpmeet. Come on here somebody! When you get ready to get married what are you bringing to the table, Ms. SistaThing, besides eyeliner and lipstick? You ain't got no savings account, all of your credit cards is charged up, and now you want somebody to be a rescue, engine engine number nine, and Zorro in your life, and he gotta come and wipe out all of your mess! The devil is a liar! God is calling you to accountability today! "It's time," as the man said last night! Get yourself together.

Bynum calls on the women to "prepare themselves" for the ministry of marriage, suggesting that if they aren't prepared, then they shouldn't "mess over the man of God." She takes them to task for not owning property, for having too many credit cards, for not having necessities like soap and laundry detergent stocked in their homes, for, essentially, being "divas" and not modeling themselves after the woman of Proverbs 31—the virtuous woman par excellence.

Bynum eventually asks someone to bring her a stack of white bed sheets that she begins to tie, one by one, around her waist. The sheets, she says, represent "layers and layers of junk" and "wrong ideas." In order to be freed from the sheets, a process is required. Bynum claims that her own processing, which was prolonged and repetitive, started only once she started praying and fasting and asking God to remove anything in her that was not like Him. It required that she enter into a life of consecration and submission. As she is saying this, she begins to remove the sheets from around her waist until they are all strewn across the stage. She goes on to say that she once had a "sugar daddy" who provided for all of her material needs but that when God "dropped her last sheet," she decided to end her reliance on men and voluntarily entered into a period of destitution:

I got poor five years ago. I had holes in my shoes. I had to go through McDonald's drive-thru to get a soda and ask for extra napkins so I could have toilet paper. I used toilet paper for that time of the month; I was poor. I'm telling ya'll I lived in the projects and I suffered because I was determined. [*She begins to cry.*] I was determined. I got tired of people kissing on me! I got tired of people with they hands in my underwear! It was too expensive! I got tired of people sleeping with me and telling people how it was! I got tired of coming to church and seeing brothers that I had been with and I couldn't lift my hands up because I knew they were saying, "I know what you like." And I told God, I said "Lord, I want to be beautiful again." I wanna—I was so ugly to myself. After that I started saying I don't wanna wear sexy clothes. I don't wanna wear—and that's why I don't. That's why I don't wear anything to show my shape or anything because I don't want nobody to choose me because I have a nice figure or I have nice legs. I want somebody to see my *heart*! I want you to be able to look at my *eyes* and see the spirit of my *soul* and *know* that I'm a *chosen vessel* and I'm a *queen*! Oh, I wish I had somebody—I just couldn't take it *anymore*! And so I was willing to become poor.

Bynum finishes telling the story of her fall from grace and what it took for her to "get her body back" by admonishing the women to recognize that until they too have been freed from their sheets and are finished being processed by God, they are not ready to be, and ultimately unfit to be, wives. To this point the enthusiastic audience has been completely captivated by Bynum. They have been on their feet encouraging her and cheering her on, even as she has reprimanded and scolded and "set them straight." But for all of their active listening it isn't until Bynum begins to close out the sermon that the place starts, as Baldwin would say, "to rock."

Part III: The Divination

The weight of the anointing that's on my life have [*sic*] severed every dead relationship that has ever been in your life *right now*. And whether you are in here and you want to let it to go or not, it's too late—I done already cut you a loose! Because I *know* what is the will of God for your life! And what you need to do, you need to get out of that place that you standin' in and run right out of it because you been cut free, it's been cut out of you, every sexual experience, every intercourse, every memory, the Lord has cut it out! It's out! You will not be able to go back to the bedroom! You will not be able to go back to the same sheets! The Lord! You better praise Him right now, He's delivering you from the memory! I don't mean stand there, I mean sho nuff praise Him! The memory! I loose you from it, I loose you from it, I loose you from it, God's got something better for you! He's got something *better*!

By the time Bynum declares that the "stench and residue" of sin has been peeled away from her listeners and proclaims to see the spirits of lesbianism, homosexuality, and perversion flying out of the walls of the arena, the audience is in a state of spiritual ecstasy. Some of the women are standing with their hands raised toward Heaven, tears streaming down their faces in a posture of worship, while others are jumping up and down and crying aloud; and still others are in a full-on run around the perimeter of the seating area. The praise going up is as communal as it is individual. At one point Bynum tells everyone in the audience to grab a neighbor by the hand and begin to praise God for that person. Later she instructs everyone to get a tissue in their hands and begin cleaning "the mess" off of themselves. Immediately thereafter she tells them to praise God for sixty seconds so that He will "detox their bodies" and then has them each grab someone and hug them—"and I mean hug 'em"—so that they will be "intertwining their spirit with a right spirit." The ninety-minute sermon finally ends with Bynum looking directly into the camera, the vast audience panned out behind her, as she decrees that she and the audience are "standing in agreement" with "the whole United States and across the water" that there will be no more sheets in any of their lives.

BETWEEN THE SHEETS

Soon after "No More Sheets" was released to video circa 1998, viewing parties of the sort I was invited to as a college student began being held throughout the country. Bynum's fan base grew as both women and men, regardless of sexual orientation or denominational affiliation, grappled with the tough-love message that was a staple of Bynum's ministry. The frank, rare-for-the-pulpit, pull-no-punches discussion of sex, coupled with the powerful rhetoric of forgiveness and healing, along with her willingness to lay her own skeletons bare, made Bynum something of a Christian phenomenon.

This was not just another finger wagging from behind the cover of a Bible, not another male preacher raining down his wrath on fallen women or another married person talking self-righteously about the ills of premarital sex. Here was a *single* woman, a God-ordained prophetess, openly admitting that she often wanted "to fall and have some sex" and that she had done so, repeatedly, in the past. She was like them. Moreover, she was giving instruction that was based on her own struggle and was the outgrowth of her own need for healing and "consecration." She understood their pain. Even as Bynum worked to codify the notion of the virtuous Christian woman into existence, she utterly exploded and complicated that same formulation. And at the same time that she subscribed to a version of what Candice Jenkins calls the "salvific wish"—an aspirational "preoccupation with propriety in the realm of intimacy" by, primarily, middle-class black women that is bound up with self-control and self-denial—she violated its tenets by exposing her "dirty laundry" and, by extension, the "dirty laundry" of all of those who aligned themselves with her message.[20]

As indicated earlier, Bynum's message is not particularly novel. According to her, the final answer to the temptations of the flesh is solely prayer and supplication. The individuals ultimately at fault for their singleness are single women themselves, and no part of the blame is meted out to their prospective (male) partners. And, per the custom of many megaministries, televangelists, and Christian teachings more generally, the emphasis on personal accountability and self-help far outpaces, and in this case totally obfuscates, any discussion of the structural, systematic, or societal bases for the very things that are said to be the reason for black women's singleness (which, it should be noted, is always discursively rooted in and read as failure), including financial insecurity, sexual promiscuity, and mental health issues. Further, there is no room in Bynum's theology, which is constructed around a no-count black female figure who is as fictitious as the welfare queen and Sapphire and Jezebel mythologies to which her rhetoric is deeply indebted, for a robust conceptualization of sexuality that not only does not revolve around marriage but does not revolve around marriage as enshrined in law (at the time "No More Sheets" was recorded) as between a man and a woman—this despite the fact that the tremendous response to "No More Sheets" attests to the acute need for just such a conceptualization. Neither is there room for a conversation about singleness that does not always see it as a problem to be solved or that takes into account the densely interconnected patterns of inequality and harm that make marriage less of an option and, in some cases, less desirable for black women and their partners.

How, then, does one respond to "No More Sheets"? How do we make sense of a message that resonates so strongly in the lives of so many black women even as it seemingly works to circumscribe those very lives? If "No More Sheets" is an illustration of a larger theological stance toward black women, and I submit that it is, what can be said about the continued presence of black women, as a critical mass, in the black church? Note the purposeful use of the present tense. Although Bynum is significantly less popular now than she once was, and although "No More Sheets" parties are largely a thing of the past, check out any of the YouTube pages that host the sermon and you'll likely find that a fair number of the comments are, one, relatively recent and, two, testifying to the goodness of Bynum's message, the substance of which continues to prevail in many a church.

In Ashon Crawley's discussion of the "black queer(ed) subject" in the black church, he gets at the "why do they remain" question, in part, by addressing the relay between the black church and the gay nightclub as first elucidated by E. Patrick Johnson.[21] Crawley suggests that the distinction Johnson makes between the church as a pre-scripted "place" where the "rhetorical discourse of the service censures and confines the body," and the liberatory "space" of the club that "frees rather than captures the sexualized body" rests on a troubling assumption.[22] Using Johnson's own example as evidence, Crawley argues that "the club, through invocation of the same language and ideologies of God and religion, can do the same sort of violence [as the black church] in another location to black queers."[23] Essentially, the notion that one can simply "escape" the oppressive logics of the black church but still maintain its cultural rites (the music, dancing, shouting, and so forth) by going to the club doesn't quite wash. That is to say, you can run from it, but you'll still be in it.[24] Moreover, Crawley contends, plenty of queer black people don't attempt to run from it at all but "continue to go to church, continue to cite it as a means for freedom and liberation."[25]

I am particularly interested in taking up Crawley's argument here because it is animated by a question of agency that is foundational to my own foregoing consideration of black churchwomen. Like Crawley, I am not content to dismiss the continued presence of my subjects in the black church as merely the consequence of false consciousness. Instead, I want to consider the possibilities inherent in the "collective enunciation of pain and burden"[26] evinced by black churchwomen in the space of the sanctuary and those spaces where black churchwomen gather in the name of sanctuary. Crawley posits the black church as a site of catharsis wherein "redressive performances of the body seek[] to repair the breaches, abjections, objections and subjections" attendant to black life.[27] The responses of black churchwomen to Bynum's message in the form of ecstatic utterances, spiritual dance, and communal praise—getting happy—are, I submit, a form of redressive performance at the same time that they are emblematic of "that power which arises from our deepest and nonrational knowledge," or what Audre Lorde otherwise terms the *erotic*.[28] That is to say, getting happy is both *backward-looking*, or concerned with redressing the pains of the past, and *forward-looking*, or concerned with striving toward a better future, even as it affirms *presence*: the shared self-connection that is, as Lorde puts it, "a measure of the joy which I know myself to be capable of feeling, a reminder of my capacity for feeling."[29]

For as much as we might critique Bynum's message and all that it stands in for, there is something to be said for what her *informality* makes possible. The communal spaces where black women can go to lay their burdens down are rare indeed, but even more rare are the instances in which black churchwomen can openly address their stigmatized sexualities. Lexi can only hint at, or use Tonéx as the scapegoat for, the spiritual-sexual "indiscretions" that Bynum lays bare. It is therefore insufficient to charge Bynum with the rhetorical oppression of black women and leave it there, because what she simultaneously lays claim to are the feelings of loss, rejection, and failure that are the unspoken detritus of so many black women's lives. In so doing, she opens up a space for *getting happy*—a space wherein the shout, an "unexplored and undesignated [site] of meaning," and the dance, "a singularly important activity in which immanently resistant communality is expressed and achieved," significantly coincide.[30] Thus what "God's decoys" help us to understand is that for all of the shortcomings of the church and church folks that could be and have been enumerated, what the *faith* gives Believers is, in the words of Baldwin, "a zest and a joy and a capacity for facing and surviving disaster that are very moving and very rare."[31]

3

THE WAY IT IS

It was the summer of 2008, and I had been tasked with planning the obligatory rite of marital passage for one of my best friends from home—the bachelorette party. Given that we were both children of the 1980s, my friend and I had decided the party would be '80s themed, complete with Pop Rocks, neon colors, Garbage Pail Kids stickers, Madonna-inspired clothing, and *Off the Wall* Michael playing in the background. So, on a muggy July evening just before my friend's wedding day, we gathered together twenty or so of her closest friends and family members, fully adorned in their throwback fashion faux pas, for a night of minor debauchery in the basement party room of a family friend.

After cutting into the chocolate-covered, penis-shaped cake, examining, demonstrating, and recounting our various experiences with the sex toys and intimate products our "pleasure party" representative had laid out before us, consuming innumerable gelatin shots, and exhausting every variant of the electric slide we collectively knew, the night finally began to wind down. Most of those gathered in the room were black women who ranged in age from their early twenties to their late forties and fifties, and they included the guest of honor's mother and her mother's long-term companion and housemate. Many of these women I knew from the church and larger black church community where my friend and I had spent the better part of our adolescent years. They were the choir members, praise-team leaders, Sunday school teachers, auxiliary-board members, and lay folks who were indispensable to our local Sunday services, as well as our sisterfriends, mother figures, and like-a-cousins who we had gotten grown with and near.

And so it struck me that this was no ordinary gathering but something truly unique, even revelatory. Although many of us had laughed, cried, worshiped, and celebrated together before in different places for different reasons, it was here, in an occasion of lighthearted prewedding ceremony, that we had created a safe space for sharing and for talking about and regaling in tales of our sexual exploits. We had gotten no small kick out of discovering just who had experimented with which sex toy or product, poked fun at our various bedroom mishaps, and been given instruction in the most pleasurable procreative techniques and positions by the more sexually adventurous women among us (and, for the record, it wasn't *just* the PYTs—pretty *young* things—providing the instruction).

Here there was no talk of respectability, of good girls keeping their legs closed, or of purity rings and chastity vows. There was no religious piety or righteous pontificating, no judgment based on past indiscretions. Here we laughed out loud without covering our mouths, we danced and moved about without regard to jiggling stomachs or overstretched jeans or flabby arms or, in some cases, rhythm. We ate messily and ran our mouths and sang off-key. It was an exhalable moment, the likes of which have been most widely and perhaps best articulated in the contemporary era in the expressions of black female cultural producers—women as varied as Mary J. Blige, Terry McMillan, Fantasia, Keyshia Cole, Jenifer Lewis, and Juanita Bynum—who subscribe to a certain kind of keep-it-real aesthetic that, regardless of concerns about artistic merit or ethicality of content, taps into and exposes the intimacies of black female life across the class spectrum,[1] including the ways in which black women experience relationship, sexual and otherwise.[2] And so it was toward the end of all of this, as those of us who hadn't taken off early were sitting around in slightly tipsy, happily worn-out contentment, that the strains of a still-familiar R&B song began to play:

Early in the morning I put breakfast at your table
And make sure that your coffee has its sugar and cream
Your eggs are over easy, your toast done lightly
All that's missing is your morning kiss that used to greet me

By the time the chorus began, anyone who hadn't already been getting her Karyn White on joined in:

I'm not your superwoman
I'm not the kind of girl that you can let down
And think that everything's okay
Boy, I am only human
This girl needs more than occasional hugs as a token of love from
   you to me

And that was it. Me and my girls went *in*. And by *in* I mean something like that slain-in-the-spirit takeover thing that corresponds to James Baldwin's notion of the sensual: "To be sensual, I think, is to respect and rejoice in the force of life, of life itself, and to be present in all that one does, from the effort of loving to the breaking of bread."[3] Here Baldwin is describing the sense of freedom that black people sometimes feel with each other, a freedom, he notes, that is particularly expressed in gospel and blues music and that emerges anywhere from the rent party to the church supper where "we have the liquor, the chicken, the music, and each other, and have no need to pretend to be what we [are] not."[4] And so we were sensual, we were *in*. Heads were thrown back, arms were thrown up, and eyes were squeezed shut as we bellowed along en masse to our girl's black-woman-love-scorned anthem.

Karyn White's "Superwoman," a single from her first and biggest selling album, *Karyn White*, released in 1988, tells of a relationship gone sour. It is the story of a woman who feels her deep and abiding love is not being reciprocated by her loved one. Although she does everything she knows to do in order to keep his affection, she can sense that something has changed, that he does not love her as he once did. The failures of the relationship are symbolized in the song culinarily: she makes his breakfast just like he likes it, but he complains about the sour juice that "used to be so sweet"; and she wonders if the complaint is directed at her. Then she fights through rush-hour traffic to make it home in time to ensure his dinner is waiting for him, but when he arrives, he says he's not hungry and would rather read the paper than talk to her. She accuses him of "going through the motions and not being fair," and when she tells him that he's changed, he "likes to think that [she's] just crazy." But she "has [her] pride," and although she "can't help but care," she requires more of him because only a superwoman, which she is not, could continue to love as she does without being loved in return.

Since the release of Karyn White's "Superwoman" in the late 1980s, a number of other female R&B artists have released superwoman-titled (to say nothing of superwoman-*themed*) songs, including Gladys Knight and Heather Headley (who both remade White's song), Kandi Burress, Vivian Green, and Mýa. One of the more popular superwoman songs was released by Cynthia "Lil' Mo" Loving in 2001 on her debut album, *Based on a True Story*, which featured "Superwoman Pt. II," her highest charting single to date. The song also featured and was the breakout hit for the rapper Fabolous, her label-mate at the time. In direct opposition to White, Lil' Mo affirms her superwoman status by claiming that although she too is "only human," unlike those other "chickenheads" she is not an "average chic" and can save her man with her "super powers"—a riff on the claim Chaka Khan made more than twenty years earlier that she could do anything her man wanted done, "naturally."[5] In the accompanying video for "Superwoman Pt. II" Lil Mo's superwoman powers are manifested quite literally, from opening a pickle jar that her much-larger, muscularly endowed male coworker is unable to open to preventing a would-be thief from taking off with a woman's purse and, finally, throwing a bowling ball so hard down the lane that she knocks down every pin in the alley. This all works in service of fortifying her claim that she has extraordinary talents in tending to her man and is further solidified by Fabolous's claim that his superwoman has saved his day and can "make [him] cum faster than a speeding bullet."

Seven years later, in 2008, Alicia Keys released her third studio album, *As I Am*, and along with it her own version of "Superwoman." Like Lil' Mo, she also declares herself a superwoman, but in Keys's version the superwoman does not exist solely in relationship to her heterosexual love interest but is representative of women who find the strength to endure despite the "state of humanity" and their own personal struggles. In her accompanying music video Keys alternately portrays four different black women, including "entrepreneur/mother/actress" Jada Pinkett Smith and "single mother/future college student" Wynter Williams, each of whom is explicitly designated a superwoman.

Karyn White's disavowal of the superwoman and the later affirmations of the superwoman by Lil' Mo and Alicia Keys are significant not only in how they differ from each other but also in light of the work of black female theorists who have argued that the narrative of the superwoman, or, as often referred to in the literature, the "strong black woman," is ultimately damaging to black women. Among these theorists the superwoman/strong black woman has typically been described as a selflessly enduring woman who takes on the concerns of everyone around her, including her children, friends, employers, lovers, and family members, without regard to her own health, happiness, or well-being. Marcia Ann Gillespie, for instance, argues that "if good women work endlessly, strive to look pretty and keep silent while serving, the strong Black woman (SBW), the ultimate heroine, is expected to bear increasingly heavy burdens while holding herself and our world up no matter the sacrifice,"[6] and Meg Henson Scales claims that the strong black woman's "most striking characteristics are her gross displays of endurance and the absence of a personal agenda. [She] lives for (and sometimes through) others, and is culturally valued in direct proportion to her personal sacrifice."[7] Gillespie and literary critic Trudier Harris both suggest that the strong black woman is often asexual, while Patricia Hill Collins and Joan Morgan suggest that what sexual agency the strong black woman does have is sublimated for the needs of her (male) partner.[8]

Generally, these theorists also contend that the origins of the strong black women are inseparably linked to chattel slavery.[9] Enslaved women were conceptualized as being extrahuman in direct juxtaposition to white women of the planter class so as to justify requirements that they produce at a level the same as or greater than their male counterparts in addition to tending to their own families and, often, the families of their white owners. This seemingly extended to slave women's emotional durability as well, as they were expected to silently suffer the selling away of their children, ongoing physical and sexual abuse, and the trauma of the auction block. Thus the very conditions that occasioned black women's extraordinary survival abilities marked them as particularly suited to surviving those conditions and justified their continued abuse.

Despite the genesis of the strong black woman narrative, a number of thinkers contend that the continued proliferation of it is a consequence of black women's "internalization" of it for protective reasons. In a discussion of literary representations of the strong black woman, Harris argues that "the portrait of the strong black woman character became the preferred representational pattern that has influenced African American writers for the past 150 years" because for many of those writers it is a counter to images of black women as sexually and morally deficient.[10] Henson Scales describes the strong black woman as a "survival tactic" used by black women to combat difficult circumstances, Melissa Harris-Perry describes it as an adaptive strategy that black women have developed in order to "battle against the vicious stereotypes of black women perpetuated by racism and patriarchy," and, similarly, Tamara Beauboeuf-Lafontant suggests the strong black woman is "a historically complex distillation of images" that black culture uses to "define womanhood" for itself.[11] Almost universally the theorists who have commented on the strong black woman recognize that while the notion that they are exceptionally strong is empowering for many black women, the narrative ultimately does black women a disservice by encouraging them to deny their own needs in the service of others and making them more susceptible to oppression and exploitation, as well as setting them up for feelings of failure and inferiority. For Harris-Perry, black women's adherence to the strong black woman narrative supports more punitive policy decisions regarding welfare recipients and drug-addicted mothers, for example,[12] and Beauboeuf-Lafontant links the strong black woman to heightened levels of depression and weight gain among black women.[13]

Under this rubric the embrace of the superwoman by Lil' Mo and Alicia Keys would almost certainly be considered problematic, even despite the artists' attempts to claim, or reclaim, the mantle of strength for, in the case of Lil' Mo, herself, and, in the case of Alicia Keys, all black women, or at least black women who meet a certain standard of acceptable behavior (i.e., they are professional successes or at least demonstrably striving to become so). Karyn White's refusal of the superwoman most clearly aligns with the scholarly backlash against the embrace of the strong black woman, but rather than attempt to malign or celebrate any particular stance toward the superwoman/strong black woman, I propose that it is perhaps more useful to attend to the conditions of White's refusal. Most significantly, White's song is neither an observation about the ills of humanity writ large nor a complaint about her day-to-day activities. She's not commenting on her career or the kids or any of the other myriad things she may have to do in order to keep the household and their lives running. The complaint is not that she's waking up in the morning to cook breakfast for her partner or that she's rushing home to cook him dinner but that he's failing to acknowledge or appreciate her efforts. She does not express her attempts at preparing his meals as he likes them as impositions but as an outgrowth of her love for him, and it is his inability to receive that love that reveals the true status of his feelings toward her. In short, she is not talking about the state of *things* but the state of her heart. In this context the superwoman is not the woman who is asked to do too much but the woman who is expected to feel too little.

What I experienced along with those other women at that basement bachelorette party those many years ago was an affective and empathetic relationship to this deep-in-love black woman represented by White in song. We had been listening to '80s music the entire evening, everything from Prince and Cyndi Lauper to Ready for the World and Roxane Shanté, and more than once someone had called out a particular tune as her "jam"; but no other song resonated like "Superwoman." This, I would argue, is because none of those other songs were cathartic in the manner of "Superwoman," which, because it is R&B (which specializes in matters of the heart), because it is *sang* by a black woman, because it powerfully narrativizes the depths of black female love, is one of those critically significant songs in the lexicon of black musical tradition for, if nothing else, its ability to conjure a profoundly emotive response from black women by speaking directly to the conditions of their hearts.

None of the party attendees expressed this form of response more profoundly than Nina, the longtime companion of my friend's mother. Throughout the evening she had been mostly quiet, sometimes nursing a drink or a plate of food, sometimes laughing along with the girls, at times humming along to this or that song, but never contributing much to the ongoing, often sexually charged, banter. Yet when "Superwoman" began to play, she, perhaps more than anyone else, was quickly swept into its lyric sensibility. She lifted her husky voice and raised her work-worn hands in homage to—something. I cannot know precisely what. I would have no more broken in on that moment than I would have disturbed my Mama during one of her silent, shivering encounters with the Divine in a church pew on a Sunday morning.

But I can surmise that Nina's abandon was testament to an *embodiment* that resounds well beyond the particularities of its specific geographic or biographic locations. By this I mean to acknowledge a thesis forwarded by Hortense Spillers, who contends that "the black woman must translate the female vocalist's gestures into an apposite structure of terms that will articulate both her kinship to other women and the particular nuances of her own experience."[14] In her discussion of the lexical interstice that structures black women's sexuality, Spillers suggests there is no greater referent for black female capacity than the black female vocalist, who "is likely closer to the poetry of black female experience than we might think, not so much, interestingly enough, in the words of her music, but in the sense of dramatic confrontation between ego and world that the vocalist herself embodies."[15] Thus, "whatever luck or misfortune the Player has dealt her, she is, in the moment of performance, the primary subject of her own invention. Her sexuality is precisely the physical expression of the highest self-regard and, often, the sheer pleasure she takes in her own powers."[16] And while it might be argued that Karyn White "fail[s] . . . to tap the surface of the larger material and sociopolitical structures of oppression in which [she is] entrenched"[17]—an argument of the sort that many people have made regarding contemporary R&B music especially—the strength of her "Superwoman" performance is not simply its lyrical content but its mode of

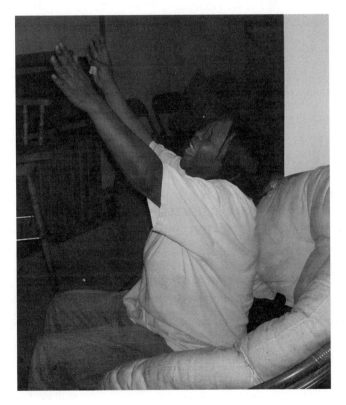

Figure 1. Nina *gone in.*

address and the extension of that modality of feeling beyond her performance via black women like Nina who, regardless of the extent of their affiliation to the song's literal message, are able to *go in* to it and find something of, and for, themselves. In fact, for black women whose lives are inextricably linked to assumptions, both right and wrong, about the nature of their insurmountable strength, finding a space to *wail* is itself a significant intervention and form of sociopolitical critique.

BLACK FEMINIST SURROGATION AND SOCIAL INTIMACY

But let me be honest. As righteous as that black women–filled space was, there were also tensions there. In a city as small as Peoria, where all the black folks seem to know all the other black folks, or at least they know someone who knows someone or can recall a family name even if not a certain individual within that family, it is bound to happen. People do not like each other. Somebody slept with someone else's somebody. Someone's best friend had a fight with someone else's sister's cousin's auntie. Someone got into it with someone on the job whom they also go to church with, who also happens to share the same hair stylist. Someone ran with a different crew in high school. Somebody fell out with such-and-so years back, and it ain't been right since. It happens. And so these types of mutigenerational, celebratory, "I ain't seen you since way back in the day," church/work/family gatherings often become sites of unexpected, and sometimes unwanted, reunion.

The point of pointing out this dynamic is not to suggest that it lessened the impact of our basement gathering—it did not—but to proffer an insight about black female social intimacy and the spaces where it is enacted. That is, these are not utopic spaces free from the tensions of everyday life or the imperfections of everyday people but complex sites wherein black social life can and does become unfettered from "the conundrums of the public sphere" that work to wrangle the passions, frustrations, sentiments, and ultimately, histories of black women into consumable, manageable parts.[18] In these spaces we can be mad but still be happy; we can laugh along with someone we despise and rejoice with our enemies, set aside our differences momentarily and pick them back up again before we leave the room. In these spaces where, as the ditty goes, everybody knows our name, our emotions are not siloed off into categorical genres but are manifestations of the deep affection, and sometimes disaffection, we feel with and for each other.

In Elizabeth Alexander's discussion of "the inner space in which black artists have found selves that go far beyond the limited expectations and definitions of what black is, isn't, or should be," or what she otherwise calls "the black interior," she asks the following question: "How do we understand 'reality' when official narratives deny what our bodies know?"[19] As a follow-up I query how in a context in which black people have been "too often prisoners of the real, trapped in fantasies of 'Negro authenticity' that dictate the only way we truly exist for a mainstream audience is in their fantasies of our authentic-ness,"[20] we might go about articulating another angle of vision—a mode of Baldwinean witness, perhaps—that gets at the complexity of black life without succumbing either to the false narratives Alexander speaks of or to the racial straightjackets that are their offspring. The intention of the question is to posit the basement sing-along as a form of what Daphne Brooks calls "black feminist surrogation, that is, an embodied cultural act that articulates black women's distinct forms of palpable sociopolitical loss and grief as well as spirited dissent and dissonance,"[21] and accordingly a point of departure for contemplating the black interior *in public*.

In contrast to Delores Williams, who refers to "social-role surrogacy" as a form of exploitation that harms black women by coercing or pressuring them to function in roles that ordinarily would have been fulfilled by other people, an argument that falls in line with scholarly critiques of the strong black woman narrative, Brooks argues that black feminist surrogation gives black women a way to "resist, revise, and reinvent the politics of black female hypervisibility in the American cultural imaginary."[22] That said, social-role surrogacy as conceived by Williams and Brooks's notion of black feminist surrogation do not contradict as much as complement each other. While Williams's focus is primarily on the relationships that black women as slaves in the antebellum period and as domestics and other laborers in the postbellum period historically had with men and white women, Brooks considers how the more contemporary post-Katrina performances of black female R&B singers Mary J. Blige and Beyoncé bear sonic witness to the lives of other black women. Thus we might conclude that inasmuch as black women sacrifice themselves to the needs of others, sometimes in ways that are willing but often in ways that are both unwilling and devastatingly difficult, they also find ways of supplementing their losses by way of their relationships to and with each other.

What I want to get at by way of the bachelorette party, then, is a consideration of the sort of translation Spillers demarcates—the articulation of kinship and experience that is the unique purview of the black woman as vocalist. Moreover, I want to consider how the vocalist-as-surrogate helps to establish or inform "a first-order discourse on black women's community," the absence of which, as Spillers contends, allows for the proliferation of black women as little more than "mythical signifiers."[23] In so doing I want to attend to the public sphere, that realm of indecipherability that has always been so tightly bound to the black female predicament. But I want to talk specifically about a *black* public sphere, what we might think about in terms suggested by Houston Baker as an "expressive and empowering self-fashioning," a reprieve from the bourgeois public sphere elucidated by Jürgen Habermas that in its very instantiation foreclosed the possibility of black participation. The black public sphere is thus a site where "what seems passively consumed as culture as a whole, whether popular, high, commercial, mass or otherwise, may be psychologically and affectively appropriated as merely a base/bass line for wildly fanciful counterpublic performances."[24]

If Stuart Hall is right that "however deformed, incorporated, and inauthentic are the forms in which black people and black communities and traditions appear and are represented in popular culture, we continue to see, in the figures and the repertoires on which popular culture draws, the experiences that stand behind them,"[25] and Herman Gray is right that popular culture is a "major site for the expression and engagement of the national (in this case American) racial imaginary,"[26] then I believe my next move, which harks back to the discussion of reality television that animates chapter 1, is an appropriate one. For whatever we might think about the form, in the contemporary moment there is no place where the lives of black female vocalists and the black women who are their primary audience converge more routinely than reality television. Since reality television made its grand resurgence in the first decade of the twenty-first century,[27] black reality television has developed into a reality subgenre heavily dominated by black women both as cast members and as viewers. Black reality television has been characterized by a number of trends in recent years, including a focus on women who are or were the partners of famous black men (*Basketball Wives, Hollywood Exes*), shows meant to cater to black Christian audiences (*Preachers of L.A., Mary Mary*), and shows set in the "black mecca" of Atlanta (*Real Housewives of Atlanta, Married to Medicine*), but there has perhaps been no more significant trend than the move toward highlighting black female music artists who have either faded from the spotlight or are in need of a spotlight in order to help jump-start their careers. While shows like *Love and Hip-Hop*, *Sisterhood of Hip Hop*, and *R&B Divas* feature(d) ever-changing ensemble casts and any number of intersecting story lines, the single artist who has emerged as the prototype for using reality television to help build a successful music career is Oakland-bred R&B powerhouse Keyshia Cole, who has starred in and received producer credit for a series of shows based on her life over the course of, as of this writing, nearly a decade. As I attempt to show in what follows, not only has Keyshia Cole sustained her music career by way of her reality television career, but reality television has also helped to situate her in a distinct surrogacy role in relationship to black women.

KEYSHIA COLE: THE WAY IT IS

The first season of *Keyshia Cole: The Way It Is* premiered on BET in 2006 as the artist was still enjoying the success of her platinum-selling debut album, *The Way It Is*, released in the summer of 2005. The album soared on the strength of its love-torn, take-no-prisoners singles "I Changed My Mind," "(I Just Want It) To Be Over," and "I Should Have Cheated," as well as her gargantuan love-it-or-hate-it ode to heartbreak, "Love." Keyshia was widely lauded for her searing, pain-filled voice and around-the-way girl demeanor, and comparisons to Mary J. Blige circa *What's the 411?* abounded. *Keyshia Cole: The Way It Is* was seemingly meant to capitalize both on Keyshia's burgeoning success and her personal narrative, which, as with Mary J. Blige, was an integral part of her initial success. From the outset Keyshia's family and background were central to the series. The first episode of the six-episode first season follows as she visits her hometown of Oakland, California, where she throws a barbecue for the residents of the neighborhood she grew up in and later holds her first local headlining concert, where many of her closest friends and family members are in attendance. As the episode opens, Keyshia tells the story of her upbringing, which is further filled in throughout the duration of the series: Her birth mother, Francine "Frankie" Lons, had seven children with seven different fathers, all of whom she eventually lost custody of because of her involvement in drug use and prostitution. Keyshia never knew her birth father, who her mother claims was an Italian man named Sal who died of cirrhosis of the liver. Frankie's other children, Keyshia's siblings, were sent to different foster homes as a consequence of Frankie's drug use, and Keyshia was raised without knowing or having relationships with most of them. Unlike with most of her other children Frankie knew and was friends with Keyshia's foster parents, Yvonne and Leon Cole, before they took her in and eventually adopted her, giving her their last name. Keyshia moved out of the Cole household and on her own when she was sixteen and bounced around for a while, using music as her "hustle." Within a couple of years she had made her way to Los Angeles, where she eventually met record executive Ron Fair, and her formal music career took off. When reflecting on her sound during a confessional moment on the show, Keyshia privileges this background, claiming, "The pain in my voice and the way I express my music comes from, you know, my mother never being there for me or, you know, me having to take care of me and my sisters or, um, you know, situations like that. I mean, it's just love in general—you're always gonna go through something."[28]

While Cole's personal and familial narrative was significant to the show from its inception, the first season of *Keyshia Cole: The Way It Is* focuses primarily on the singer herself and on following her as she maneuvers through the music business, be it in meetings with music executives, working in the studio, preparing for concerts, or interacting with fans. But a change in the show's direction is forecasted in the final episode of the first season with Frankie's introduction, when Keyshia and her older sister, Neffeteria "Neffe" Pugh, go to visit her at the Malibu Conservation Camp, where she is imprisoned for a drug-related conviction. By the time the first episode of the second season aired in the fall of 2007, Frankie had been released from prison and relocated to Atlanta along with the rest of the family by Keyshia, and hers is the first voice heard as the episode begins. The opening scene shows the family—Keyshia and her management team, Frankie, and Neffe and her three children—sitting together in the living room watching the first-season finale in tears as Frankie recounts her time in prison and the painful experience of giving Keyshia up when she was four years old. This moment is indicative of the shift the show makes in its second and third seasons, which are less about Keyshia as an individual artist and more about her family dynamic, particularly the tempestuous relationship between Keyshia, her mother, and her sister. The description of the show on the jacket of the second-season DVD collection is straightforward about its focus:

> Her mother Frankie is coming home . . . from prison. Her sister Neffe has some serious sibling issues. And for hip-hop superstar Keyshia Cole, that's just the beginning of the emotion-charged real-life drama in this hit BET series. Through therapy sessions, heated discussions and tough love, the women work to rid themselves of past demons and strengthen the ties that bind them. The series inspires, motivates and digs deep into the heart and soul of the R&B star who, at the end of the day, just wants the love of her family.[29]

From a commercial standpoint the shift in focus makes sense. Keyshia, the industrious up-by-her-bootstraps young singer who loves and seemingly wants to empower everyone around her, is significantly more interesting when she is surrounded by her hot-headed big sister, who uses alcohol as a mechanism for coping with a past that includes rape and prostitution and who in the second season of the show finds herself unexpectedly pregnant with her fourth child by a man other than her husband, and her high-strung mother, who is trying, often unsuccessfully, to rebound from a twenty-year crack addiction and the difficult consequences it has had on her relationships with her children. From the standpoint of black people concerned about the negative implications of such characterizations on black representation more generally, however, *Keyshia Cole: The Way It Is* and *Frankie & Neffe*, the popular duo's spin-off show that aired for one season in 2009 and returned for a second season in 2015, added to the then-ongoing backlash against BET for its consistently controversial programming and to mounting frustrations over depictions of black women on reality television as uncontrollable, angry, and prone to conflict.[30] Keyshia herself contributed to the antagonistic responses aimed at Frankie and Neffe in particular. In advance of premiering *Keyshia & Daniel: Family First*, a reality show that focused on her life with her new husband and son, on BET in 2012, Keyshia actively distanced herself from her mother and sister, citing the need for "serenity and peace" in her life and her dissatisfaction with the direction they took *Frankie & Neffe*, stating that she would reconnect with her family when they could "show the world that you can change for the better."[31]

But rather than get mired in an inherently unwinnable debate about the merits of black reality television or the lack thereof, I want to take seriously the relationship between Keyshia, Frankie, and Neffe as a form of surrogation that in its enactment of relational and familial harmonies and disunities, of black female social intimacy, registers black women's joy and pain in significant ways. Indeed Joseph Roach's formulation of surrogation as a process of substitution contingent on memory and forgetting, that is, culture, that can never accurately duplicate what it professes to represent— which is to say that performance is always already grounded in inadequacy—turns questions of meritocracy on their heads. While in the present instance the anxieties inevitably generated by surrogation sometimes take the form of debates about negative or positive valuation, "this process is unstoppable because candidates for surrogation must be tested at the margins of a culture to bolster the fiction that it has a core. That is why the surrogated double so often appears alien to the culture that reproduces it and that it reproduces. That is why the relentless search for the purity of origins is a voyage not of discovery but of erasure."[32] In other words, black reality television, especially a show like *Keyshia Cole: The Way It Is*, is an artifact of the very sociocultural landscape it reproduces, and the backlash against it that purports to name itself as a concern with the "truth" of black life doubles back on itself in the avowal of a fiction that it is something other than what it is. And "what it is" can neither be won or lost nor contained within oppositional frameworks, and it is more elaborate than the modes of capitalistic (re)production that would attempt to rein it in but can never finally succeed in doing so.

By way of example I want to consider a segment of one of the family therapy sessions that became a staple of the second and third seasons of *Keyshia Cole: The Way It Is*. This first session was attended by Keyshia; Frankie; Neffe; Keyshia's assistant, Ronique; her manager, Manny; and their therapist, Dr. Wilson, and it aired in part during the second episode of the second season.

> DR. WILSON: What feels like it's the problem in the family? Why are you in tonight? Keyshia, what's the matter?
> KEYSHIA: I've been adopted my whole life. Um, since I was about two years old, my mother has always been on drugs for as far as I can remember. You know, it's just a weird thing with me, like, I kinda backlashed—like how Neffe does me now—I kinda did that to my foster parents. Like I didn't want them to love me because my mother

didn't love me. And I don't know if Neffe doesn't want me to love her because our mother didn't love her. But, I don't know, you know, I'm trying to come up with things and scenarios to figure it out.

DR. WILSON: You're looking for answers.

KEYSHIA: Yeah, I don't know exactly what the problem is.

FRANKIE: I was the problem at first. I'm not in denial. *I was the problem.* They haven't forgiven me yet, neither one of 'em, for what I've done to them.

NEFFE: She hasn't been forgiven because we would get mad and we would say things that penetrate her heart from what she didn't do in the past. I have done that purposely so that she could feel what I felt when she wasn't there. And I think that's why we lash out.

FRANKIE: "You can't tell me nothin'." "Where was you?" "You wasn't there." They still say that to me.

KEYSHIA: "She wasn't there" is a true statement. They expect me to disown my foster family—

FRANKIE: I don't want you to!

KEYSHIA:—because we're together now. Us building a relationship *now* is okay, but I can never forget my past.

FRANKIE: Okay, that means you'll never forget what *I* did in *my* past if you can never forget your past. Listen to what you saying. They were my family before they became *your* family.

KEYSHIA: And you should be thankful—

FRANKIE: I'm always thankful! It's just some things you say—

KEYSHIA:—because without that I woulda been a little worse off.

FRANKIE: No, without that you would still be what you are today because it's God's will.

KEYSHIA: Right. And it's called streets—you know, when the streets get a hold of you? Look at Neffe. Because the streets got a hold of her— Mother, she did not have a foster family to care for her. She had to run to the streets. She ran to dudes. All kinda things happened to Neffe while you was gone. Some of the things that happened to you.

FRANKIE: While my mother was gone. So it's a curse. It was a family curse.

KEYSHIA: Right. So thankfully I had a foster family that cared for me, that took me to church, that got me to know God as good as I know

Him right now, because without Him I wouldn't be here. You're right.

FRANKIE: I went to church with that family before *you* did, Keyshia.

MANNY: You wanna defend yourself by not letting it happen again! It already happened, so you did wrong, you're tryna—

FRANKIE: I said I did wrong, but you're not gonna rub it in my nose!

MANNY: Yes, we are!

FRANKIE: I'm not a dog! 'Cause it's a mistake I made, and I corrected it, and you're not—Keyshia not, Ronique, and Neffe—nobody's gonna make me feel guilty for the rest of my life about nothing!

NEFFE: How I'ma rub it in your face and I was right there along with you?

FRANKIE: I did it! Let's get past it!

NEFFE: How can one get past it if you keep bringing it up?

FRANKIE: Ya'll either forgive me or you don't. That's all I wanna know, from Neffeteria and Keyshia.

DR. WILSON: What about you letting you forgive yourself?

FRANKIE: How can I forgive myself if the people around me won't forgive me?

DR. WILSON: You know, they say it starts within. You gotta go within or you go without. So I want to ask you, have you made that step to allow yourself to start with you first?

FRANKIE: I—you know what, it's probably I don't know how.

DR. WILSON: You don't. Okay, I appreciate your honesty.

FRANKIE: I don't know how.

DR. WILSON: Okay.

FRANKIE: I don't.[33]

This exchange is indicative of the individual grievances that motivate each woman as well as the collective trauma that structures their relationships to each other. Frankie remains haunted by her past, which includes her confessed drug addiction and other just-beneath-the-surface skeletons that probably went hand in hand with her addiction, as well as the time she spent away from her children, and this reveals itself most starkly in her frustration with her daughters' seeming inability to forgive her and her corresponding inability to forgive herself. But over the course of the series Frankie's reckoning with her past reveals itself in other ways as well, including in her hostility toward Keyshia's adoptive parents, who she feels tried to turn Keyshia against her, in her continuous string of significantly younger and allegedly abusive boyfriends, in her tendency toward very inebriated and very public emotional outbursts, and in her stated desire to hear her children call her "Mama" and her grandchildren call her "Granny" and to be treated as such. To this last point Frankie says that for someone who was "MIA" for so long and who is just learning how to mother effectively, "being a mom is harder than being clean on drugs."[34]

In Neffe's case the lingering effects of, among other things, watching and sometimes being with her mother as her drug use escalated (Frankie notes that during their youth she spent more time with Neffe, her oldest child, than with all of her other children combined), her mother's prolonged absence *as a mother*, being sexually abused by a family member when she was a child, struggling with the decision of whether to abort her fourth pregnancy, and going through the separation and divorce process with her husband of more than seven years after he cheated on her with her first cousin all contribute to her narrative as a broken woman in need of healing. Late in the third season of the show Neffe has a major emotional breakdown when she is taken to meet with Bishop Eddie Long (who has since settled lawsuits with several congregants over allegations of sexual and financial abuse) for a counseling session at his church, New Birth. She says she is embarrassed about being a "backslider" in need of forgiveness, and after Long tells her that God has forgiven her, he then asks her whether she has been able to forgive herself. Neffe's response is to say, "I don't know if I did." Still, by the time the session is over, Neffe apparently has a better perspective on her life and is able to proudly proclaim, "You will absolutely see me being a soul winner for my Heavenly Father because that's the transition He put me in right now."[35]

Other than the therapy sessions, the moments when the themes of transition and healing are most urgently sensed come when Frankie and Neffe talk directly to other black women about their lives. In the second season the two women visit Mary Hall Freedom House, a center that provides shelter and related assistance to women recovering from addiction in Atlanta, where they testify to the experience of Frankie's drug use. Afterward, as women in the audience are speaking to their own experiences, Frankie says she "feels something" in the room. At that a woman collapses into tears, and Frankie leads a group prayer on the woman's behalf as they collectively weep, lift their arms heavenward, and cry out to God. As the scene ends, Keyshia, who was not present at the event but whose scenes are cut in showing her working in the studio as it is happening, says, "I've done everything that I can do myself. The rest is on them. Life is what you make it. *I* made my life this way. *I* changed my life. I did what I needed to do, so I just hope that they can do the same thing, whatever that may be. They family, I'ma back them up regardless. I just hope it's the best because I want the best for them."[36]

In a discussion of the Emmy-winning courtroom drama *Judge Judy* and similarly styled courtroom television programs, Laurie Ouellette argues that reality television is a significant site for the proliferation of neoliberal constructions of citizenry in the contemporary moment. Using Judith "Judy" Sheindlin's model of no-nonsense, tough-talking, from-the-bench moralizing as an example, she states that "*Judge Judy* and programs like it supplant institutions of the state (social work, law and order, welfare offices) and, using real people caught in the drama of ordinary life as raw material, train TV viewers to function without state assistance or supervision, as self-disciplining, self-sufficient, responsible, and risk-averting individuals."[37] Ouellette suggests that Judge Judy, by establishing herself as the normative, responsible citizen and the typically undereducated, working-class litigants who come before her as largely deficient and abnormal, aids in the state-sanctioned regulation of those individuals who are seen as drains on the system due to their alleged failures in taking personal responsibility for their lives.

In an important follow-up to Ouellette's essay Anna McCarthy contends that reality television often operates as a "neoliberal theater of suffering," a realm of excess in which pain and trauma are key to understanding the processes of self-organization that govern the subject. Rather than indict reality television for its exploitation of personal suffering, McCarthy suggests that the utilization of traumatic experience on reality TV can be understood as a useful strategy of civic expression that potentially exposes the limits of neoliberalism. She posits the reparative makeover show—in this instance she focuses on *Random 1*, a series that aired on A&E from 2005 to 2006—as a site wherein the neoliberal project that Ouellette describes is seemingly altruistic rather than disciplinary. The premise of *Random 1* is that its two hosts, a "tracker" and a "social worker," travel the country looking for individuals who are in need of assistance of some sort. They then work alongside their mobile support staff on behalf of these random individuals to solicit the help they are in need of, but without spending any money. In the episode McCarthy describes, Bruce, a homeless man with a troubled past and a history of alcoholism, is granted a much-needed prosthetic leg upon the assertion by one of the hosts that "with the leg no longer an obstacle [he] can decide if and when to rebuild his life."[38] *Random 1*'s bottom line, then, is that it is only interested in helping those people who are fully invested in helping themselves, not in providing welfare to those who may become dependent on it. Yet, McCarthy observes, Bruce still does not have a job by the end of the show, and the lasting impression is that the initial door *Random 1* has opened is probably the only one that has been or will be opened and that Bruce has in fact "donated his trauma" to those who will benefit from telling his story and who are able to walk away feeling good about themselves for their acts of goodwill.[39] Accordingly, the onus is placed on Bruce to feel good about the burden of responsibility that has been placed on him with the granting of his new leg, a burden that he dare not reveal at the moment when he is expected to perform on camera his joy at his benefactors' generosity. McCarthy sums up the function of Bruce's traumatic experience in this way:

> Indeed, from the eye-level perspective of individual stories—the perspective from which people actually make, and watch, television—the *failure* of *Random 1* to make much of a difference in Bruce's socioeconomic circumstances seems far more salient than its assertion that it is trying to do so. Trauma, I want to suggest, remains unassimilable and unrationalizable, ultimately ungovernable. The program is not, ultimately, a makeover but rather an extended mediation on the nature of making over—encompassing governmentality's imperative to make oneself over and the "making over" through which traumatic memory returns, again and again, to constitute its subject afresh, in the rawness of the past moment, frozen in relation to others and to history.[40]

Trauma exceeds the boundaries of regulation. Just as governmentality is working to make rational subjects, trauma exposes the instability of rationality. It "names experiences at the limits of rational knowledge and sovereign selfhood, exposing the challenges that terrifying experience pose for any coherent expression of history, memory, and individual autonomy."[41] The countless stories of suffering told by reality television are therefore instructive because, if we look closely, they reveal the extent to which so-called democracy is undercut by socioeconomic inequality and disenfranchisement.

In relation to *Keyshia Cole: The Way It Is* I submit that Keyshia often functions as neoliberal interventionist. Whereas the stories of Frankie and Neffe are revealed as messy and dysfunctional, Keyshia holds herself out as the rational daughter and sibling who generously extends her love and compassion, as well as her money, to her family in order to help save them from themselves. While the details of Frankie's and Neffe's indiscretions and shortcomings are lavishly exposed over the course of the series, Keyshia's past is neatly contained within the narrative of the abandoned daughter of a drug-addicted mother. Though she occasionally mentions the significance of her adopted family in her life, she more often talks about how hard she had to work to make something of herself, by herself, and holds herself up as a model that her family should duplicate.

The tension between Keyshia's makeover ideology and Frankie's and Neffe's making over is readily apparent in one of the first scenes of the second season, just after Frankie and Neffe have moved into Keyshia's house in Atlanta. Keyshia sends Frankie off to have her hair done and to be fitted for a set of dentures, as all of her teeth were removed while she was in prison following a beating she suffered at the hands of the father of one of her children prior to her arrival there. The scene is bookended by a toothless Frankie, her head covered in a scarf as she talks about the adjustments she's trying to make living with Keyshia, and a "new and improved" Frankie, her hair and nails freshly done and her smile made perfect, talking about how it feels to be "rehabilitated." But in between, as Frankie sits in the salon chair having a hair weave sewn in, she breaks into tears when addressing the rules Keyshia has set in place, one of which is that the women can have no male visitors at her home. "I hope it work out," Frankie says. "'Cause, guess what, I don't wanna feel locked up. So I gotta do me. 'Cause I do feel like I'm still in jail. And I don't 'pose to feel like that, hunh?"[42]

The scene is edited to suggest that Frankie is primarily upset about the rule against male visitors, which may be the case, but rather than dismiss this moment as the inconsequential ramblings of an emotional, and perhaps ungrateful, Frankie, I want to consider its importance in illustrating the disruptive force of trauma and the limitations it exposes. Frankie's meltdown at the very moment she is being made over into the image of the respectable mother figure Keyshia has always wanted suggests the price to be paid for respectability. Here the question of value that I take up more explicitly in chapter 5 looms large. What does it mean to go from being in the life—a term that, in this case, most explicitly refers to involvement in street prostitution and illegal drug use but that is also, as I discuss later, the articulation of a certain kind of refusal—to being implicated within a system that denies the very plausibility of that life and, in fact, sets you in direct opposition to it? Here it means not simply that Frankie cannot have male visitors when she would like but that her entire (way of) being has been upended. And despite Keyshia's most sincere efforts her financial generosity and self-help rhetoric and therapy sessions cannot fix the rupture that has been Frankie's, and by extension Neffe's, entire life. The ongoing drama between the three women, which spills out into their *real* real lives when Keyshia publicly distances herself from her mother and sister, attests to this inadequacy. Rarely an episode goes by when Frankie and/or Neffe are not erupting—crying, arguing, screaming, fighting—often with, or at, each other. Still, the most poignant moments of the show are Frankie and Neffe's as well: Frankie jumping into Neffe's arms when Neffe arrives at the correctional facility to visit her; Neffe collapsing into tears as she tries to explain why she feels so strongly about Frankie not remaining in abusive relationships ("She been so broken and hurt and drug through the dirt for so many years. . . . And now that I see that she's a strong black woman, I don't want anyone to take that from me"); Frankie and Neffe in Oakland visiting with Ya Ya, Frankie's mother and Neffe's grandmother (whom Neffe calls her "Sojourner Truth") and discussing her role in their lives; and both of them openly sharing their stories with other women affected by drug abuse at an Atlanta recovery center.

What Frankie and Neffe thus give us, if I can be so bold as to suggest they give us anything of substance, is a look into the intimate sociality of black female love in all of its unbridled messiness. Certainly this is no pure thing, as the exigencies of production often compel excess performance. But black women know something of both excess and performance and what is held in the exchange between the two. If, as Lindon Barrett argues, "blackness is positioned as excess in relation to a more 'legitimate' and significant presence known as whiteness," and the singing voice constitutes "the preeminent sign of the production of cultural value in African American communities,"[43] then we might argue that the singer, at the moment of performance, (re)articulates the *necessity* of the excessive black body. That is to say, the black singer, in this case the black *female* singer, both exposes and counters the delegitimization of excess, thereby "mark[ing] a point of exorbitant originality for African American cultures and expressivities."[44] Keyshia indirectly speaks to this "alternative organization of sociality"[45] when she notes how indebted she is to her mother and her scarred background for the tonal quality, or pain, in her voice. For inasmuch as Keyshia attempts to hold herself apart from the excesses of her mother and sister, it is in her performance that the distance collapses and that, however inadvertently, she "interprets through form"[46] the abject positionality from which she otherwise attempts to hold herself apart.

4

BABY MAMA

In 1987 and 1988 Peoria led the nation in the percentage of births to unmarried black girls and women in cities with populations over one hundred thousand.[1] Growing up in Peoria, I heard some version of this statistic repeated numerous times, but it was not until much later that I learned that it was, in fact, a fact. Not only did I learn of this fact, but I learned that the publication of it *as fact* caused no small amount of hysteria in my hometown because it had, as one local journalist somewhat hyperbolically summed up the community sentiment, "put Peoria County on the map as the teen birth capital of the nation."[2]

I first started becoming aware of my city's "pregnancy problem" when I was in sixth grade, though I was not particularly attuned to the statistical or sociological bases of it at the time. That was the first time one of my schoolmates, another sixth grader, showed up to school pregnant. I didn't know her well—I don't know that I ever had so much as a single conversation with her—but I do remember that she became quite the scandal among us eleven- and twelve-year-olds. She was very quiet and usually by herself, no one I was friends with seemed to know much about her personal life, and it was not uncommon to see one student or another stopping her in the hallway before or after our classes to ask her some, I'm sure very inappropriate and thoroughly invasive, question about her burgeoning belly or the circumstances leading up to it. I personally never tried to engage her in conversation, but she did remain for me, who at that time was still pretty much petrified by even the idea of sex, something of an enigma. It's not clear to me what happened to her after she had the baby. One day she was there, the next she wasn't, and to my knowledge she never returned to that particular school again. But by the time I graduated from high school six years later, pregnant schoolmates had become part of the routine. It was no longer a surprise to see this or that girl waddling from class to class, her rounded belly leading the way. The pregnant girls became part of our day-to-day lives; more often than not they would leave to have their babies and return weeks later, their bodies reconfigured, pictures of new baby in hand. Every now and then one of the boys would show up to school proudly displaying his hospital wristband, proof that he had recently become a father. Even I had become a godmother after one of my good friends gave birth to "our" daughter during our freshman year of high school.

Between 1990 and 1998, the years I was in middle school and high school, the percentage of pregnancies to unmarried black women in Peoria ranged anywhere from second in the nation (1991 and 1998) at the high point to fifteenth in the country (1997) at the low point.[3] Indeed, during this same time period the areas of the country that routinely had the highest pregnancy rates among unmarried black women were largely concentrated in the rust-belt cities of the upper Midwest and Northeast. These included St. Louis (which ranked first most often and is located about 170 miles south of Peoria), Gary, Erie, Pittsburgh, Milwaukee, Rockford, South Bend, and Cleveland, among others. This geographic trend of high percentages of unmarried black mothers, specifically black teenage mothers, being concentrated in the postindustrial heartland continues today in spite of the fact that these same areas have some of the lowest rates of pregnancy for white teenagers and state-specific teenage birthrates are generally highest across the southern United States.[4]

Hindsight (and aging) being what it is, I know now that the news of Peoria's "epidemic" of unwed mothers, which was largely read as a problem of black teenage pregnancy, which in turn was largely read as a problem of young black girls run amok, was fodder for a number of social and educational initiatives meant to alleviate said problem, including some that touched me directly. This included the abstinence program I was involved in at my home church. Although my church apparently was not one of them, in 1996 several local churches, most of them with predominantly black congregations, received small grants for programming designed to "combat" teenage pregnancy as part of a strategic alliance between the Heart of Illinois United Way, a local charitable nonprofit organization, and local religious institutions.[5] Clearly many city officials and residents thought churches and religious teaching on sexual propriety, which most commonly took the form of scriptural mandates against any and all extramarital sexual activity, should have been at the forefront of determining solutions to reining in the problem of unwed mothers. Consequently, what felt to me at the time like just another random church program I was duty bound to participate in was actually the culmination of heightened anxieties about the seemingly unchecked sexuality of young people and the outgrowth of a nationwide trend toward faith-based sexual education programs.

Another initiative purportedly designed to reduce the numbers of black teenage mothers that I was involved in during high school was a college-readiness program called College-Bound Assistance for Excellence that, according to one local headline, was meant to "help girls avoid the pregnancy trap."[6] This headline, which I came across while conducting research for this book, was news to me. For me the program involved a small, tightly knit group of girls coming together every so often under the tutelage of our beloved director, Mrs. Erma Davis, to discuss any number of issues that might come up in relation to applying for and attending college. Our interactive sessions included everything from learning proper study habits to demonstrations in dorm-room cookery to lectures in female reproductive health. While sexual education and pregnancy prevention were addressed occasionally, those issues never felt like the core of the program, and while I perhaps knew it at the time and had since forgotten, I was surprised to learn later, again from local newspaper archives consulted in conjunction with this book, that any of us who became pregnant while in the program could have been expelled. Luckily, then, none of us did get pregnant—at least while we were in the program. Because at least three of us who went through College-Bound together did get pregnant shortly after graduating from high school or while in college. So much for avoiding the "trap."

This is not meant to suggest that College-Bound failed. To the extent that the program was about preparing us for the college experience, it was a success; most of us did go on to graduate from college in a timely fashion, including at least two of those who became pregnant following high school. And whether or not this was a stated goal of the program, what it also did successfully was create a safe space for black high school girls and our black female mentors to gather together to share a common experience toward a common goal. I still remember College-Bound as a warm spot during what were, for me, very difficult high school years, and I remained friends with some of the girls well past the conclusion of the program. Further, many of us who participated in the College-Bound program throughout its duration continued to check in with Mrs. Davis occasionally and update her on the goings-on of our lives until her death in 2013.

It is an odd thing to look back on your life and realize you were part of a targeted population that you did not know was being targeted and to have to come to terms with the knowledge that the threat you always at least suspected you posed extends even to something as seemingly mundane as your reproductive *capacity*. (I return to this important word, *capacity*, later.) What I didn't know then that I know now is that I came of age during the height of the still-palpable teenage pregnancy wars, when the problem of poverty was increasingly being seen as the problem of young unmarried mothers, of all races, and the tongue-clucking over "babies having babies" was, at best, a concern over the consequences of "pathological" teenage sexuality on teenagers themselves and, at worst, a lingering concern over the effects of Ronald Reagan's mythologized welfare queen on the citizenry's tax bill.

This "war" came to a head in Peoria in February 1994 when, after a year of investigative work, the local newspaper, the *Journal Star*, ran a five-day series of articles titled "Unwed Parents: Delivering the Future" that was meant to bring attention to and serve as a call to action about the city's disproportionately high rates of (black) teenage pregnancy. Although it was never explicitly talked about as a "black problem," unwed and teenage pregnancies among white girls and women in Peoria have historically been at or below the national average, and it was clearly the release of data about the numbers of black unwed mothers in the city that initiated the sense of crisis. This was made strikingly evident the very first day of the series when the articles and their accompanying photographs confirmed that the "unwed parents" at issue were predominantly young black girls. The series's coverage began on the front page of the paper all five days, and the image on the front page on the first day showed a sixteen-year-old black girl named Denise holding her newborn daughter for the first time as her mother and best friend look on. Images of this same girl run throughout the day's coverage: in one she is shown, still pregnant, standing in the hallway during summer school along with several other black teenage girls, another one of whom is also visibly pregnant. In another she is shown, her new baby beside her, "signing up for a government-subsidized baby formula program" along with her seventeen-year-old friend, who is also the mother of a new-born baby. But the most contentious photo ran under the headline "Teen Motherhood Runs in Family" and features Denise as she is in the process of giving birth. She is seen lying in a hospital bed flanked by her sixteen-year-old best friend (who, the article tells us, is pregnant with her second child) and her older sister (who, the article also tells us, is the single mother of five children born out of wedlock), her hospital gown pushed up around her midsection, her knees bent up toward her chest, her legs suspended in the air as she holds onto her knees and bears down in the midst of a contraction. A white nurse sits at the end of the bed pressing into the heels of Denise's feet as she peers into her fully bare, gaped-open legs monitoring the progress of her labor. The baby's father is not present in the photo, we're told, because he was in jail at the time of the birth.[7]

A little more than a week after the launch of the series, Linda Henson, the white photographer who took the offending photograph, responded in print to the outrage it had provoked among some black residents, a number of whom were leaders in the community, who felt the *Journal Star*'s coverage of the issue was negative and demeaning toward black people, painted teenage pregnancy as essentially a black problem, and was particularly shameful because it had run during Black History Month.[8] "Get mad," Henson countered, but get mad *at the problem*: "If an image I shot of a 16-year-old suffering through the pain of childbirth causes you to confront an issue, I know I have done my job as a photojournalist."[9] Henson and her colleague Shari Mannery, a black journalist who also contributed to the "Unwed Parents" series, argued that residents were "ranting and raving over a photo" and overly concerned about the image of black folks and their own embarrassment when they needed to have been more concerned with finding solutions to the "disgraceful" numbers of (black) Peoria-area teenagers having babies.[10] This sentiment that something needed to be done about the high (unwed, black) birthrate and that it needed to be done urgently was the impetus for the reformulation of a community task force on teenage pregnancy several months later by the Heart of Illinois United Way—which had established the first such task force in 1986—that was charged with "searching for a better cure to perhaps the area's biggest social problem."[11] Both the 1986 and the 1994 versions of the task force were hampered by internal and external divisions and, depending on whom you believe, effected more or less change to the *rate* of (black) teenage pregnancy, which, it is

Figure 2. Denise with friends during a learn-while-you-earn program offered to teenagers through the local school district the summer before her daughter was born. (Linda Henson/*Journal Star*)

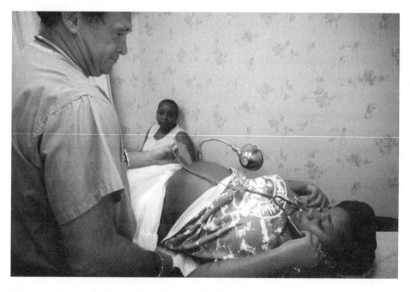

Figure 3. Denise during a doctor's visit. (Linda Henson/*Journal Star*)

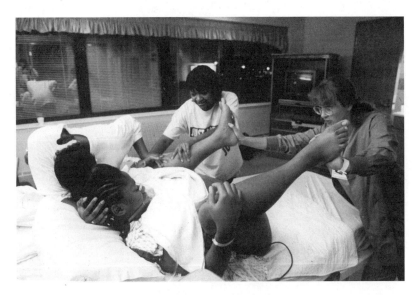

Figure 4. The birthing picture of Denise that ran during the first day of the *Journal Star*'s "Unwed Parents" series. (Linda Henson/*Journal Star*)

Figure 5. Denise with her best friend, LaToya, and her mother immediately after giving birth to her daughter, Dasia. This picture ran on the front page of the *Journal Star* on February 6, 1994, the day the "Unwed Parents" series began. (Linda Henson/*Journal Star*)

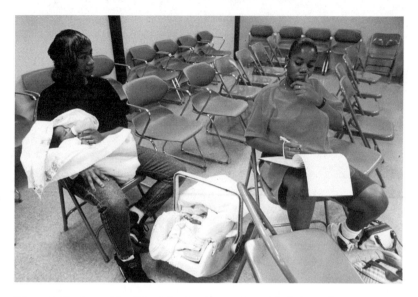

Figure 6. Denise and her friend Stephanie, together with their newborns, signing up for a baby formula program run through the Peoria City/County Health Department. (Linda Henson/*Journal Star*)

important to remember, was always the central issue—despite the hand-wringing over, and some residents' sincere concern about, the precarious *lives* of (black) teenage mothers themselves.[12] And nothing characterized the underside of this debate better than the *Journal Star*'s dubious attempt at "humanizing" the issue through its "Unwed Parents" series.

THE BLACK GROTESQUE

In an important consideration of the relay between racialization and discourses of value, a subject that I take up more pointedly in chapter 5, Lindon Barrett draws on philosopher Mark Taylor's contention that the grotesque body is "an exemplar of '[t]he free activity of play [that] enacts rather than represses [the] paradoxical coincidence of presence and absence'"[13] to argue that, in the United States, the grotesque is necessarily embodied by African Americans.[14] As the point of passage between inside and outside—indeed, as certain strains of black intellectual thought would have it, as the very being-ness that makes inside and outside possible—the grotesque black body delimits a society that is "seething with [its] presence,"[15] even as it goes not just unspoken but, as Barrett suggests, *unthought*. In other words, "the privileged presence of whiteness in the U.S. landscape depends upon an absence understood as the grotesque and negligible African American body."[16] It is precisely because the African American body is "understood" as grotesque that its centrality to "universal" U.S. culture is so profoundly *unthinkable*. In the end, the ruse of the grotesque is the willing disavowal of black social and intellectual life.

The fallout from the birthing photo verifies Barrett's consequent claim that "interest in the 'never individual' life and 'interstitial' nonidentity of 'grotesque' black bodies never easily enters U.S. culture, or U.S. contemplative thought, of any period."[17] I suggest, then, that the offending photo holds no simple answers and that its offense can be neither explained by nor neatly written off as moralistic black respectability politics or the yearn for positive black representation. Inasmuch as the body of a laboring black woman-child became, in Peoria, Illinois, in 1994, the hypervisual site on which public shame(ing) was both visualized and enacted, that same body is, by historical, cultural, and social extension, a comment on the sexual regulation of black women's bodies that endures into the contemporary moment.[18] Further, whereas Barrett suggests that the female body in "its moment of giving birth" is particular in its grotesqueness, I suggest that the "grotesque" birthing photo is merely pretext for a black grotesque that is not confined within any particular moment or set of moments but is, to borrow a term from Frantz Fanon, the "epidermalization" of the alternative.[19] This it to say that the birthing photo became the scapegoat for the real offense, which was not simply the image of a black teenage girl deep in the throes of labor but the corporeal imaging of an alternative (read: abnormal) sociality rooted in and sustained by blackness.

While it might be easy enough to see how the laboring black body was used as "a resource for metaphor"[20] in the tug-of-war between the *Journal Star*, which saw it as the embodiment of a cultural pathology in grave need of fixing, and black residents, who, at least in some instances, saw it as a source of embarrassment and marker of degradation—not to mention those residents, white and otherwise, who saw it as *the* source of moral and social decay—what is perhaps less obvious is the way that same body, and the actors it stands in for, comments on the uses to which it is put. Barrett

Figure 7. Nineteen-year-old Sean Boone was featured in the second day of the "Unwed Parents" series along with his one-year-old son, also named Sean. (Linda Henson/*Journal Star*)

provides us with a concept to aid in contemplating this endeavor, which he terms "bla(n)ckness": "a *blankness* informed and confirmed by an asymmetrical relation sustained with *blackness* (among other things)."[21] For Barrett, bla(n)ckness evades a concern with the assumed polarity of whiteness and blackness—it is in fact suspicious of the very notion of boundaries that such dichotomization implies—that might consign the current discussion to the types of narrow morality debates that played themselves out in the pages of the *Journal Star*, in favor of a more nuanced threefold analysis. According to the (dis)logics of bla(n)ckness,

> Traditional discourses are radically questioned. They are exposed as grotesque and unthinkable themselves, by exposure of the moments at which they abrogate their own premises, moments at which they transgress the very boundaries established for their self-definition and dominance.
>
> In the light of these self-riddling moments, untraditional and competing discourses are more readily apparent, for, exposed as arbitrary, dominant discourses revealed as not uniquely rigorous, nor coherent, nor rational, nor moral, and so on, set in relief not only their arbitrary internal principles but also the arbitrariness of their relations to Other discourses over which they are merely dominant and not unquestionably superior in rigor, coherence, rationality, morality, and so forth.
>
> The violence, formalized as the boundary, first setting the dominant and untraditional discourses in an oppositional relationship becomes an issue newly open to scrutiny and newly open to reevaluations of its apparent neutrality. The boundary is the register of violence marking itself otherwise; it (seemingly) fixes itself "when [open] force gives way to ideas" or, more plainly, when physical and social force is recast as the force of reason and evidence, assuming in this way an ontologically different (and neutral) status, a status in which boundaries appear as independent factors in the oppositions they set in place and maintain. One must see, on the contrary, that this independent status of the boundary depends entirely on the sanction of the dominant discourse and its stabilizing opposition. The dominant discourse slyly redoubles itself as dominant position and neutral boundary, thereby slyly casting as symmetrical (as two counterposed elements distinguished as a boundary) what is in fact unsymmetrical (two elements counterposed to one in a hostile systemic configuration).[22]

One of the most significant contributions of Barrett's conceptualization of bla(n)ckness is that, in the vein of Barbara Christian and others before him who have contested "the race for theory," it affirms that "African Americans have always been grappling with the most difficult and perplexing of intellectual matters."[23] It helps us to understand how black folks theorize about and make sense of their lives and the structures that enable and are enabled by them. In the case at hand it is young black teenage mothers, read through the "grotesque" black female body in labor, who lay bare both the limitations of the dominant discourse—a discourse that relies on those same "others" in order to stake its claim—and the capacity of black social life.

BLA(N)CKNESS AND VALUE

Numerous social scientists have already warned us that the relatively recent hysteria over teenage pregnancy is both excessive and misdirected.[24] They argue, for instance, that what President Bill Clinton, who in 1995 could have been echoing the laments of Peorians made a year earlier, called "our most serious social problem" apparently was not deemed much of a problem at all during the 1950s, when the rate of births to teenagers was at its historic high and was, in fact, twice what it had been in previous decades. It was not until the late 1960s and early 1970s, when teenage birthrates were actually *declining* nationally, that teen pregnancy and teen parenting began to emerge as significant social issues, the consequences of which could purportedly be felt by the majority of Americans. Kristin Luker argues that the congressional hearings over the ultimately failed National School-Age Mother and Child Health Act proposed by Senator Edward Kennedy in 1975—which would have designated $30 million each year for three years to be used by state agencies for "services for school age girls and their children" had it passed—initially established the parameters of the issue in the national conversation and influenced the policy debates for years to come. The hearings, wherein the concept of "teenage pregnancy" was publicly formulated for the first time, established that teenage pregnancy was a "serious and growing problem" linked to school dropout, poverty, and "an increasing dependency on welfare and other community resources." Although the 1975 act did not pass, three years later, when Senator Kennedy held a second set of hearings around his newly proposed legislation, the Adolescent Health, Services, and Pregnancy Prevention and Care Act, the notion that teenage pregnancy is a leading cause of poverty had essentially become doctrine, and the 1978 act passed with the support of the Carter administration, as well as strong congressional support.[25]

A number of factors contributed to the growing sense of crisis in regard to teenage pregnancy. For one, although the rate of teenage births declined in the aftermath of the post–World War II baby-boom years, a period during which *all* American birthrates increased dramatically, the number of *unmarried* teenage parents began steadily to increase. While a significant majority of teenagers who became pregnant prior to the 1960s were married at least by the time their babies arrived, as early marriage became both less desirable and less tenable, single parenthood became a more viable option. This in turn created an increased demand for public assistance and other services benefiting single mothers and their children. Thus, "although unmarried women in their twenties and early thirties actually had a much higher rate of nonmarital births than those age fifteen to nineteen, what initially caught the attention of policymakers and the public was not the changing *rates* of nonmarital childbearing per thousand unmarried women, but the changing *ratio* of nonmarital births—the percentage of all births born to unmarried women."[26] Organizations such as the Guttmacher Institute bolstered the alarm by publishing data that purported to highlight the harms associated with early pregnancy and childbirth. One of their tactics was to draw comparisons to the lower pregnancy rates in other European and Anglophone countries but without acknowledging the long history of early family formation in the United States or that the issue had to do more with the declining desirability of marriage than it did any sort of newly deviant behavior on the behalf of teenagers.[27] Also at issue was a new demographic measure that came into effect with the legalization of abortion in 1973. The "pregnancy rate" combined the live birthrate and the abortion rate so that even though birthrates were actually declining, the pregnancy rate was increasing as teenage abortion rates increased. So, to the extent that there was a "problem" emerging, it actually had to do more with the uptake in abortions among teenage girls—who have always accounted for less than a third of all abortions performed—than it did with teenage pregnancy itself.[28]

This primary concern over the marital status of teenage mothers, most of whom, significantly, are eighteen- and nineteen-year-old legal adults by the time their babies are born, was evident in the "Unwed Parents" series.

Except for a 170-word piece published on the third day of the series, which was titled "Marriage No Way to Escape Poverty" and which was neatly nestled beside an article about how one black father's criminal history kept him away from his children and another about the stress of single parenthood on a black mother who had two children by two different fathers by the time she was seventeen, the *Journal Star* couched its coverage of the issue entirely in terms of the ills of out-of-wedlock childbirth and the failure of teen mothers to get married. By framing the issue in this way, the Peoria debate, like the national debate, created the impression that teenage pregnancy was on the rise and assumed that marriage was a cure-all, thereby obscuring the problems attendant to early marriage (and marriage more generally) and denying the plausibility of alternative familial arrangements.[29] It also revealed that as much as the hysteria over teenage pregnancy was, and is, about the economic repercussions to taxpayers, it is simultaneously centered on a conservative religious ethic that mandates sex as for marriage only and therefore leaves little room for a discussion of the robust sexual lives and needs of young people. Consequently, the debates about what to do about teen pregnancy, in Peoria and elsewhere, often become hampered by tensions between those who advocate the need for abstinence-only education and those who would like to see teens have increased access to resources such as sex education, contraception, and abortive procedures. Whatever side of the line advocates fall on, however, the common ideological denominator—the line, so to speak—is that teenage pregnancy is a rampant social problem in desperate need of a solution. And the "problem" of sex becomes its defining characteristic.

Given the particular social and political climate out of which the problem of teenage pregnancy first emerged, it has, by and large, been laid at the feet of young black girls and women:

> Thus, in the 1970s and early 1980s the data revealed a number of disquieting trends, and teenagers became the focus of the public's worry about these trends. More single women were having sex, more women were having abortions, more women were having babies out of wedlock, and—contrary to prevailing stereotypes—older women and white women were slowly replacing African Americans and teens as the largest groups within the population of unwed mothers. These trends bespeak a number of social changes worth looking at closely. Sex and

pregnancy had been decoupled by the contraception revolution of the 1960s; pregnancy and birth had been decoupled by the legalization of abortion in the 1970s; and more and more children were growing up in "postmodern" families—that is, without their biological mother and father—in part because divorce rates were rising and in part because more children were being born out of wedlock. But these broad demographic changes, which impinged on women and men of all ages, were seen as problems that primarily concerned teenagers. *The teenage mother—in particular, the black teenage mother—came to personify the social, economic, and sexual trends that in one way or another affected almost everyone in America.*[30]

While it is true that black teenagers have historically represented a disproportionate number of teenage pregnancies and out-of-wedlock births, what is also true is that black teenagers are disproportionately affected by poverty.[31] Though seemingly obvious by now, this is a crucial point. Researchers have increasingly found that much of the governmental and private funding that has gone into curbing teenage pregnancy in the belief that it would consequently make a significant dent in the levels of poverty and inequality has produced "remedies" that are often minimally effective, when they are not altogether counterproductive. Here cause-and-effect is fatefully misinterpreted. Rather than being a *cause* of poverty and social disadvantage, teenage pregnancy is more rightly understood as an *outcome*, or marker, of poverty and social disadvantage. The notion that by drastically reducing the teenage birthrate the poverty rate will subsequently be dramatically reduced disregards the reality that the majority of teenage mothers are impoverished *prior* to getting pregnant and that waiting a few more years to have children until they are, say, in their early twenties does little to nothing to ensure they and their children will not (continue to) face social and economic disadvantage.[32] According to one study, even a dramatic decrease in the teenage birthrate would result in only a moderate decrease in welfare spending, since many of those same mothers would still need assistance even if they put off childbearing by several years.[33] Another study suggests that if all teen mothers delayed childbirth, expenditures for public assistance might actually *increase* slightly.[34] The benefits of marriage in this regard are limited as well since the fathers of impoverished children are often as economically and socially disadvantaged as the mothers, if not more so. Seen in this way, the solution to the all-important question of how to reduce welfare spending becomes something of an either/or proposition: either do something to eradicate the conditions of poverty itself (and not merely its consequences), or tell would-be welfare recipients to stop having children, period. Candice Jenkins articulates the reality of this latter proposition in her discussion of the continued resonances of stereotypes of black women:

> Like other specters created during slavery, Jezebel reappears in contemporary American culture through such figures as the "welfare queen," the image of an unwed and unfit black mother feeding voraciously on white tax dollars and producing hordes of literally and figuratively "dangerous" black children. I say figuratively dangerous because while some of the fear of such children grows from the sense that they will become, as adults, the urban criminals who allegedly threaten the safety of American streets, another part of the "danger" of these children is found in their (assumed) numbers—and the accompanying sense that they have the power to engulf whites with a particularly destructive blackness. In other words, the mythological black welfare mother, because of her reproductive capacity, is painted as the very "agent of destruction, the creator of the pathological, black, urban, poor family from which all ills flow."[35]

In one of the few long-term studies of teenage mothers that has been conducted in the United States, sociologist Frank Furstenberg followed a group of young mothers in Baltimore, most of them black, over the course of more than thirty years, from 1965 until 1996. One of the things he found was that by their midforties mothers who had children in their teens were doing significantly better than he and most other researchers would have expected based on foregoing analyses, holding that "we must consider the distinct possibility that early childbearing has only a modest effect, or conceivably even no effect at all, on the mothers' prospect of having a successful educational, occupational, or marital career."[36] He bases this claim not just on the problem of selectivity—that is, researchers still have not been able to adequately account for the demonstrable affects of both individual and group dynamics, including social climate, family structure, cognitive ability, and mental health, that adhere prior to teen mothers becoming pregnant—but also on his finding that while teen mothers do often have a very difficult time in the years immediately following the births of their babies relative to their peers, they tend to rebound in the long term. To say they "rebound" is not to suggest they necessarily become "successful" in normative terms but that they generally end up financially and socially on par with similarly situated women who delay having children until later in life.[37]

Another social scientist, Arline Geronimus, contends that given culturally adaptive fertility-timing norms "in communities such as high-poverty, urban areas, where income is low and precarious and healthy life expectancy is uncertain, the vitality of the community may be enhanced by early childbearing norms *coupled with* a normative family structure that is multigenerational and extends responsibility for children's well-being beyond the biological parents."[38] In other words, Geronimus is staking a claim for the legitimacy of teenage parenting, particularly within black communities, that acknowledges the role of those communities in its legitimation. Here "legitimacy" does not mean unequivocal support but the recognition that certain black familial and communal structures are inherently designed, for reasons both logical and logistical, to support those people and practices that might otherwise be deemed *il*legitimate. Consequently, the boundary between the legitimate and the illegitimate is effectively blurred by the black mother-child, who is, ultimately, the consummate social rupture.

An article in the fifth and final installment of the "Unwed Parents" series features a seventeen-year-old mother named Chia Freeman. Chia was a sixteen-year-old high school sophomore when she gave birth to her son, and the article, titled "Mom Tried to Help End a Pattern," notes that Chia's mother was a teenage mother of three, which "helped lead to a drinking problem she fought for years." In a move characteristic of the "Unwed Parents" series as a whole the article also notes that "men, women, girls and boys throughout [Chia's] extended family are parents of babies born out of wedlock," which problematically and probably intentionally conflated unwed parenthood with teenage parenthood. Still, although Chia was not married, she was living with her boyfriend, the baby's father, who took care of their son while she was in school. The following is an excerpt from the article:

After finding out about the pregnancy, Freeman's mother encouraged her to consider abortion. Freeman decided against it, in part because she knew that whatever happened—even if she and [her boyfriend] Allison ever broke up—relatives would be there to help care for the baby.

She didn't view being an unwed teen-age mother as a problem. "I consider it normal," she said. "There are kids right now who are 14 and having babies. It's really common in the 90s."

"Marriage is a bigger step," she continued. "When you're getting married, you're making a commitment. Marriage is good because you're setting a good example for your children but . . . it doesn't have to be the dad who is there with the mom and the child. It could be the mom and the grandmother—as long as the mom has support."[39]

Four days later Chia's comments were used against her in a follow-up editorial written about the "Unwed Parents" series:

"If the purpose of your feature on unwed teen-age mothers was to engender feelings of understanding and pity, I'm afraid it failed to do so with this reader," a Peoria man wrote to our reader Forum last week.

"My reaction was simply one of anger and disgust over those irresponsible promiscuous deadbeats who are sucking the welfare system dry."

That sums up rather succinctly the angry reaction of many of our readers. Indeed, there was even a little something to make bleeding liberals blush with fury in the five-day series on unwed pregnancy. Among our personal favorites was the comment from the 16-year-old girl who considered parenthood at 14 "normal" then went on to say that she hadn't married because "when you're getting married, you're making a commitment." Like parenthood isn't a commitment?

The girl's 19-year-old boyfriend, the father of her child and an unemployed high school dropout, then poured gasoline on the fire by saying he didn't plan to return to school, but still hoped to get a job managing other people—"something that doesn't take a lot of work but where you can still make good money."

What planet are these people living on?

We know they're young and young people sometimes say and do stupid things. But when you consider that those local teens have put a price tag on their irresponsibility of $30 million a year, more than half District 150's education budget, your temperature is bound to rise a bit. And when you consider that nationally the cost is upwards of $34 billion, excluding public housing, special education and other social services—as much as we spend on agriculture and the space program combined—it's enough to make the guy who's working his butt off at $7 an hour go ballistic.[40]

The article goes on to provide a list of initiatives it suggests will help solve the problem of teenage pregnancy, starting, unsurprisingly, with welfare reform and ending with an assessment of Hollywood's role in "promoting promiscuity as a glamorous lifestyle for which no one pays the price."[41] In between, in a nod to, perhaps, moderation, it acknowledges that jobs must also be part of the solution. An earlier article in the "Unwed Parents" series had briefly reported that it was during the recession of the 1980s, a recession that uniquely and severely impacted Peoria and devastated its black residents, that the unwed birthrate began to rise substantially.[42] Indeed, as noted at the outset of this chapter, it was during this period that the pregnancy rate among unwed black mothers in Peoria reached the national apex. In the decade between 1980 and 1990 the area lost more than seventeen thousand manufacturing jobs alone—jobs that typically paid well and did not require a college degree—and black workers lost the greatest share of those jobs.[43] Although the national median income for black households actually rose in the 1980s, in the state of Illinois it fell by 3 percent, and in Peoria County it fell *42 percent* between 1979 and 1989. The median income for white households in Peoria County fell 15 percent during this same time period.[44]

On the one hand, the *Journal Star* editorial acknowledges this link between financial insecurity and the rise in unmarried birthrates by advocating the pressing need for well-paying jobs, but it takes it away with the other hand when it claims, "By the same token, young people and their parents have an obligation to acquire the skills they need to be employable. The public school doors are open for anyone who wants to walk through them. It's not Caterpillar's fault that someone is 16 years old and can't read."[45] There is no discussion of how economic crises also affect public education, particularly when taking into account that the "young people and their parents" being targeted here are primarily situated in neighborhoods that, even in the best of economic times, house the most underfunded, underresourced schools in the city. Further, it assumes that if these same young people would only take some initiative and go to these underfunded, underresourced schools and "learn to read," then they would be well positioned to accept the jobs that would, presumably, be freely offered to them if the economic conditions were such that Caterpillar and other employers could afford to do so. It also assumes, as do the readers whose opinions it quotes, that these "young people and their parents" are content simply to live off the dole and take no accountability for their actions, their own lives, or the lives of their children.

To this last point, in a follow-up piece published in the *Journal Star* less than a week after the initial editorial, Chia wrote in to the paper's reader forum to defend herself and her views:

> I am one of the unwed mothers interviewed for the "Unwed Parents" article.
>
> I recall reading in Monday's newspaper about one particular man's comments referring to my interview. First of all, some of these "deadbeats who are sucking the welfare system dry" are students. I, myself, am a high school student, and I also receive welfare assistance. But I also worked at a part-time job for four or five months in which I had to go directly from school and not return home until after 10 p.m.
>
> This started interfering with my school work and my relationship with my 15-month-old son. So, being the intelligent person I am, I decided that my school work and my son were more important. So I am no longer working.
>
> My main point is that everyone on welfare is not "sitting back and sucking the welfare system dry." I also want to add that I said pregnancy at the age of 14 is normal because it basically is. This does not mean that I feel it is right. All of the interviews that were made should prove that teen-age pregnancy is normal.
>
> I feel really bad that the "unwed parents" articles disgusted so many people, mainly because this is a major issue and problem in the 1990s. Instead of everyone being disgusted, they need to do something other than talk about it and be disgusted. Things need to be done, such as clinics put in schools, sex education classes starting in fifth grade, and other things that will teach the youth how to prevent teen-age pregnancy.
>
> I am very proud of my baby's father because he was, and still is, there for me and our baby.[46]

What Chia accomplishes here, both by her writing and the example of her life on display, is a full-throated enunciation of the specter of bla(n)ckness. To briefly index Barrett's outline by way of Chia, (1) traditional discourses are radically questioned; (2) untraditional and competing discourses are more readily apparent; and (3) the structure of violence that undergirds the purported oppositional relationship between the traditional, or normative, and the untraditional, or nonnormative, is exposed. Chia acknowledges familial arrangements in which the raising up of children extends beyond the two-parent household and is shared among a network of kin who, among them, endeavor to support those children, financially and otherwise, even in the event that one or both of the parents does not or cannot support the children themselves. Obviously these types of extended kinship networks (and in using the term "kin" I mean to gesture toward relationships that extend well beyond the biological) are now and always have been critical to the operationalization and sustenance of much of black life, and Chia recognizes them as foundational to the "normalcy" of teenage pregnancy.

To suggest teenage pregnancies and the kinship networks that support them in black communities are "normal" is not, as the *Journal Star* would have it, the "stupid" commentary of a young person who does not know any better or, worse, just will not do any better, but the affirmation of a modality of life that refuses to be regulated by the poverty, oppression, and marginalization that are the conditions of its possibility. This is to say, the "problem" of teenage pregnancy looks vastly different from Chia's perspective than it does from the perspective of the *Journal Star* and a strong contingent of its readership. For Chia the issue is primarily one of *resources*. She does advocate a range of services she believes would help prevent teenage pregnancy but does so from the perspective of someone who recognizes that early parenthood can be a struggle, not because young parents are "irresponsible deadbeats" but just the opposite—because they want the same types of things for their children that older parents want for theirs but, due to their age and consequent social positioning, are significantly less likely to be able to access, at least initially. Thus her concern is not that young mothers are unable to be good mothers, nor does she seem to view early motherhood as the social death sentence some advocates would make it out to be— indeed in her *Journal Star* profile she is quoted as saying that her grades actually improved after her son's birth because it was then that she felt she "had something to work for"[47] (which, if the many similar anecdotes I have heard to this effect are any indication, is not an uncommon phenomenon and one that should be seriously considered).

Further, Chia's view of marriage is consistent with research finding that teenage mothers and their parents are increasingly unlikely to see marriage as a pregnancy cure-all, recognizing instead, often from experiences among their own families, that hasty marriages between young parents rarely succeed and can easily compound the difficult situations such parents already face. Here again the perspective of teenage mothers is instructive. They do not avoid marriage because they lack a moral compass—when what is considered "moral" is configured by way of the terms and structures that animate normative "commonsense" discourses about the family—but because their sense of morality instructs their often high regard of marriage. According to Furstenberg's account of the children of the teen mothers he began following in 1965:

> In contrast to their grandparents, who regarded marriage as an inevitable and desirable decision to make when facing a premarital pregnancy, and their parents, who viewed it with a certain degree of wariness but believed it was a necessary condition for success, this generation adopted a different perspective: marriage was a privilege to be achieved or earned by dint of education and economic accomplishments. Marriage has become a conditional transition to be undertaken only when justified by strong indications of success. The formidable barriers to marriage that have been erected over the years are taken by young people to be a warning not to enter marriage without the requisite resources.[48]

BLACK CAPACITY AND THE REPRODUCTION OF NON-VALUE

In *The Arcane of Reproduction* Leopoldina Fortunati suggests that the value of reproduction to capital is that it functions as *non-value*. She posits the family, or housework, and prostitution, or sex work, as the two main sectors of reproduction under capitalism, arguing that in precapitalist economies, "while as a slave or serf, i.e., as the property of the master or the feudal lord, the individual had a certain value. But as a 'free' worker under capitalism, the individual has no value: only his or her labor power has value. Thus the other side of the transition from pre-capitalist slavery to capitalist 'freedom' is a total stripping of value."[49] Capital is thus a dualistic structure in which production, or the waged labor of "the factory," is separated off from reproduction, or the nonwaged labor of "the home," but "the real difference between production and reproduction is not that of value/nonvalue, but that while production both *is* and *appears as* the creation of value, reproduction *is* the creation of value but *appears otherwise.*"[50] Despite this apparent separation, reproduction is both a precondition and condition of production—production could not occur *but for* reproduction, and production is integral to the process of reproduction. And because reproduction must be seen as a natural force on which capital has no bearing (workers are "free" to have children as they choose without regard to the market), the commodity in question is no longer the individual but the commodity contained *within* the individual, which is to say, "the *capacity for production* has exchange-value."[51] This illusory dichotomy quite obviously has distinct ramifications for male workers, in whom the capacity to *produce* has been primarily developed, and female workers, in whom the capacity to *reproduce* has been primarily developed. Both men and women are exploited under the terms of capitalism, but because women's productive capacity is subordinated to their reproductive capacity, they are *super*-subordinated by capital. In sum, "it is the positing of reproduction as non-value that enables both production and reproduction to function as the production of value"[52] because, in the first instance, the commodity is no longer the individual as it was in preceding modes of production (e.g., chattel slavery) but the labor power of the valueless "free worker" and, in the second instance, because reproduction is seen as a "freedom" that produces other valueless "free workers."

According to this schema, Fortunati argues, reproduction is primarily organized by the interdependent sectors of the family (i.e., a natural force of, or service to, social labor) and prostitution (i.e., an unnatural, or criminal, force of social labor). In the case of both housework and sex work, the relation appears to be between individuals satisfying reciprocal consumptive needs, but both occur, in actuality, between the female worker and capital through the mediation of men, again due to the female worker's capacity to reproduce—which cannot be valuated as such but is indirectly waged via labor power. Consequently, "the capitalist organization of interpersonal relationships" requires, and in fact structures and substantiates, the normative family model, particularly among the "appropriate" classes, and affects even those who are considered, under this model, too young to initiate the familial unit for themselves:

> In capitalist society all generations are affected by capitalist organization of individual sexual relationships. The opportunity to have such relationships has always been tied in to the possession of, or access to money or goods which provide the individual with a means of maintaining him/herself. Broadly, those who don't work have no right to sex, not only because the sexual politics of capitalism have always upheld the concept of "sex as reward" for the workers, but also because capital has always tried to ensure that those capable of reproducing are also capable of maintaining any eventual children. Thus non-adults are formally denied the opportunity of having any unwarped, open relationships. However the struggles of children and youth have been so consistent and so radical that they raise the doubt that this vetoing of sexuality for non-adults has ever been very effective. Today capital is finding it increasingly difficult to impose its will on non-adults, with the exception perhaps of very young children.[53]

If, in the case at hand, we take the lead of Saidiya Hartman and Frank Wilderson, the generalization of the category of "woman" that grounds Fortunati's assessment might give us some pause. For they and others, including, as indicated earlier, Barrett, have asked us to consider the "position of the unthought," the black nonsubject who cannot neatly figure into the rhetorics of marginalization or subordination because it is in fact the "unthought" who brings those systems into alignment.[54] Wilderson contends that the distinct enabling conditions of blackness are not alienation or exploitation, as could be said to be the case with other groups of people who are white or nonblack people of color (with Native Americans constituting a liminal exception), but accumulation and fungibility, "the condition of being owned and traded" ("Being can thus be thought of, in the first ontological instance, as non-niggerness, and slavery then as niggerness").[55] Consequently, white capacity is contingent on, actually "parasitic" on, black incapacity, where "capacity" is understood as "a kind of facility or matrix through which possibility itself—whether tragic or triumphant—can be elaborated."[56] In other words, blackness is denied the very thing it calls into Being, and the life that is lived within blackness (i.e., black Beingness) "is not analogous to those touchstones of cohesion that hold civil society together."[57]

Bearing this is mind, I want to suggest that the single black teenage mother—variously called the "promiscuous deadbeat," the "welfare queen," and in more contemporary popular parlance, the "baby mama"—is in a distinct position to help us reckon with the question Fortunati enables: *What does it mean to reproduce, or have the capacity to reproduce, non-value?* According to the "touchstones of cohesion that hold civil society together," Chia and Denise visually, textually, and materially represent the grotesque point of passage that "proves worthy of little, if any, speculation beyond ways to maintain its subjugation."[58] But what if we consider that Chia, Denise, and similarly situated black women evince a radical disregard for, or reorientation of, "civil society"? That even if "civil society" disregards their disregard, that precisely *because of* such disregard, they enact a refusal that cannot be subsumed within the logics of death, social or otherwise? What if we were to say that the baby mama, as the manifestation of a fugitive subjectivity that reproduces non- or negative value is a "queer subject" who by "throwing into crisis and into relief our most precious and pervasive ideations of the normative, along with the ideological, economic, and political apparatuses in which the violences of normativity operate,"[59] is, consequently, the very articulation of black social life?

Some prevailing strains of stereotype discourse might suggest that the *Journal Star*'s "Unwed Parents" series was problematic because it was a degrading representation of blackness and that the fault for this misrepresentation might be assigned to any number of actors, including the *Journal Star*, the *Journal Star*'s reporters, or even the "unwed parents" themselves. Regardless of to whom they laid blame, this line of thinking resonated in the dis-ease that many black Peorians had with the series and was most clearly encapsulated in their response to the birthing photo. I submit, however, that the birthing photo was actually the least *theoretically* offensive of the *Journal Star*'s offerings and that what was really at issue, for black and nonblack Peorians alike, was not the "grotesque" black body on display but the imaging of a "grotesque" alternative theory of normative sociality.

A black boy smiling down at his toddler son. Two pregnant black girls standing in their high school hallway among other black girls, seemingly enjoying themselves. A black girl celebrating the birth of her first child with her sixteen-year-old best friend, who is pregnant with her second child, and her older sister, the mother of five children born out of wedlock. Another black girl defending the unemployed, high school dropout, black father of her child, while simultaneously defending her own claim to motherhood. *These* are the scenes that offend. *Here* is where the terms get revalorized. *This*, the absence and refusal of shame, is the black grotesque embodied.

Outside of all bounds—young, female, unmarried, poor, black—with the capacity to produce more of the same, the black teenage mother poses a threat that precedes and exceeds the field of representation and exposes the fault lines of capitalist (re)production. She codifies an unthinkable way of Being, a countermythology, that alleges no commitments to law or order. And it is in this, her will toward rebellion, that she "marks a crisis for dominant signification."[60]

5

IN THE LIFE

In April 2007 I was a twenty-something-year-old doctoral student at the University of Southern California. I was at the predissertation stage, still taking classes, at the moment when I had some ideas but didn't quite have a *project*. Whatever my project was going to be, I knew it was going to have something to do with black women, representation, and media. That much I knew. But what I also knew in early 2007 was that there was this other thing I wanted, actually *needed*, to write about. I didn't think that this other thing had much of anything to do with my "real" project, I just wanted—needed—to write about it so I could understand it, so I could grapple with it in a way that I'd been unable to up until that point.

And so over the course of two graduate seminars I began work on this other thing, this "side project," that took me emotionally, spiritually, and even physically back to Peoria. For it was in this, my midwestern home-town, the consummate American city where it must "play" if it's going to "play" at all, or so they say, that ten black women between the ages of twenty-nine and forty-five had either turned up dead or gone missing between 2001 and 2004. Of these nine occurred over a fifteen-month span between July 2003 and October 2004. One of these women, Tamara "Tammy" Walls, I had known personally, had sung alto with in the young-adult choir at Prince of Peace Missionary Baptist Church where both of our families had been faithful members for many years. Nine similarly situated black women dead or probably dead in less than two years in a city with, at the time, a black population of approximately 28,000 and an overall population of fewer than 113,000. It was, it seemed to me, an outrage. Or at least it should have been. Yes, of course, these were black women, black women who were all said to be involved in prostitution and illegal drug use, and clearly the lives of such women rarely receive much media attention, especially when the story is about how to *save* their lives as opposed to how we can go about holding them responsible for every social ill we can conceivably (or inconceivably, as the case may be) pin on them. But, still, *all those women.* It seemed to me that if anything involving the epic and continuous violence perpetuated against black woman was going to become a national headline, it was this.

But it was not to be. It wasn't to be in 2003 or 2004 while the body count was steadily increasing and black residents throughout the city were in fear for their lives and the lives of their loved ones. It wasn't to be in early 2005 when a local white man, Larry Dean Bright, confessed to killing eight of the women, to doing drugs and having sex with them, strangling them, and dumping their bodies around the city or, in the case of four of his victims, burning their dead bodies in a makeshift fire pit he had dug behind his home. It was not to be in May 2006 when that same man was sentenced to life in prison without the possibility of parole after entering a plea deal that allowed him to escape the possibility of the death penalty in exchange for his full confession.[1] There was never a national call to justice, cable news networks never dedicated segments to debating or contemplating the case, prominent activists never climbed up on their bully pulpits on behalf of the victims or their families, major newspapers never sent their journalists to cover the court proceedings. What attention the case did receive was very localized, and even that was often delayed, incomplete, or inaccurate.

But it was while I was in the midst of my early research and writing about the Peoria case, on April 4, 2007, to be exact, that the injustices experienced by a group of black women did manage to draw national attention. On that day, the day after the Rutgers women's basketball team lost the NCAA national championship game to Tennessee, radio "shock jock" Don Imus raised the national ire in momentous fashion when he referred on air to the Rutgers team as "some nappy-headed hos" who, co-opting terms from the 1988 Spike Lee film *School Daze*, he and his fellow commentators imagined as the "jigaboos" to Tennessee's "wannabees." While it is unnecessary that I spend much time here recounting the Imus debacle—plenty was said about it at the time, and at least one book has already been written about the incident[2]—suffice it to say that Imus and company's comments made folks *mad*, especially black folks, especially black folks whose bread and butter is responding to racial animus, both real and perceived. They were so mad, in fact, that their advocacy ultimately led to the cancellation of *Imus in the Morning* several days later (though he returned to airwaves with a reconfigured version of the show less than a year later).

Although I was unaware of it at the time, it was at that moment that my project was truly birthed, that it became something more than a basic treatise against the ill treatment of black women by the media (which it had previously been in grave danger of becoming) and became about a different kind of inquiry altogether. Because it was during the Don Imus dustup that I first became invested in talking about what Hortense Spillers has called the black intramural and Elizabeth Alexander talks about in terms of interiority—with thinking about how blackness functions from the inside out, about its commitments, its investments, and its sense of itself.[3] And the reason for this turn initially had to do with the nature of the advocacy that occurred on behalf of the Rutgers women, particularly as it played out in national media. The typical defense at the time held that the women of the Rutgers women's basketball team did not "deserve" to be called nappy-headed hos because they were, in fact, *not* nappy-headed hos. They were instead, as their coach, C. Vivian Stringer, put it, "the best this nation has to offer . . . young ladies of class, distinction. They are articulate, they are gifted. They are God's representatives in every sense of the word."[4] Similarly, NCAA President Myles Brand and Rutgers University President Richard McCormick issued a joint statement that read in part, "It is unconscionable that anyone would use the airways to utter such disregard for the dignity of human beings who have accomplished much and deserve great credit."[5]

While I, like most of the activists, journalists, and commenters advocating on the Rutgers women's behalf, did not then and do not now know any of them personally, I have no doubt that Stringer's description of them was accurate. Nor did I find any fault with the impulse to advocate forcefully on their behalf (when said advocacy was actually about the greater good and not simply an exercise in self-aggrandizing pontification of the liberal variety). What I did then and do now have some serious misgivings about, however, is a conceptualization of worthiness (e.g., what one "deserves") that fundamentally relies on the same formulation it is purportedly at odds with in order to make its case for itself. Here the argument that proceeds along the line of unmitigated disavowal inherently functions to avow the very thing it purports to strain against, and the outraged claim that the Rutgers women were not nappy-headed hos suggested that it wasn't that particular configuration of terms that was the problem as much as it was that those particular women were being associated with it. Given that I was at that very moment being inundated with the deaths of black women, many of whom had been involved in drug use and prostitution—which is to say that they were the most literal embodiment of the disreputable nappy-headed ho—I wondered if what I was contending with was not simply a question of media incompetence or disregard but a deeper and more abiding question about the nature of black sociality. What, I wondered, does it mean that one man can be nationally berated for referring to a group of black women as nappy-headed hos, while literally hundreds of black women have been and are being viciously slaughtered one after the other across this country—indeed, as my research progressed, I came to know that the Peoria murders were not an isolated incident as I had originally believed but one of more than sixty serial murder cases that have occurred in the United States since the early 1970s wherein black women have been the sole or primary targets[6]—and their deaths raise nary a peep and that this silence is at least partially as a consequence of their affiliation with that same representative configuration?

This, I think, is no easy question. It is not one that can be responded to fully by recourse to media discrimination—that is, we do not know because the media does not tell us. Neither can it be gotten at by way of stereotype discourse, which maintains that the nappy-headed ho is a racist trope of the white imagination that depicts black women negatively and must therefore be rallied against. While I believe both of these things to be true—the media does discriminate and does therefore make it difficult for us to know about instances of social injustice (and thus commits its own social injustice), and the nappy-headed ho is indeed a racist trope in need of dismantling—what is at stake here is an inquiry into the very conditions of black social life, conditions that allow for the articulation of something like a nappy-headed ho while they simultaneously, in their profuse instantiation, reject the nappy-headed ho as ontological possibility. Here is James Baldwin on this very thing:

Aunt Jemima and Uncle Tom are dead, their places taken by a group of amazingly well-adjusted young men and women, almost as dark, but feriociously literate, well-dressed and scrubbed, who are never laughed at, who are not likely ever to set foot in a cotton or tobacco field or in any but the most modern of kitchens. There are others who remain, in our odd idiom, "underprivileged"; some are bitter and these come to grief; some are unhappy, but, continually presented with the evidence of a better day soon to come, are speedily becoming less so. Most of them care nothing whatever about race. They want only their proper place in the sun and right to be left alone, like any other citizen of the republic. We may all breathe more easily. Before, however, our joy at the demise of Aunt Jemima and Uncle Tom approaches the indecent, we had better ask whence they sprang, how they lived? Into what limbo have they vanished? However inaccurate our portraits of them were, these portraits do suggest, not only the conditions, but the quality of their lives and the impact of this spectacle on our consciences.[7]

Baldwin posits that the outright repudiation of our mythological forebears comes with a price, and in his discussion of Richard Wright's crowning achievement *Native Son* (1940) he suggests that it is in the character of Bigger that we can most clearly see this price being paid. In Wright's attempt to use Bigger as social commentary on the black condition, to use him to say something about the lived experience of the black, he runs right back into the problem of Bigger that he is writing against. Bigger does not, in fact cannot, exceed the terror that calls his own being into existence because he is no more than a reproduction of that same terror. Because black life in *Native Son* is unhinged from itself, because it is missing *tradition*, the shared experiences and ways of life that establish blackness as something more than terror or isolation or death, because Bigger is a symbol without relationship, either to himself or to others, blackness becomes, in this view, as debased and pathological as it was always already assumed to be. And it is in this severe cutting away from black life, what is sometimes talked about as "progress," that Wright's project fails. It is ultimately a surrender to the catastrophic American image of the black, "and when he has surrendered to this image life has no other possible reality."[8]

To buy into the logic of, in Wright's case, the violent black buck or, in our case, the nappy-headed ho (and here "buying into" takes the form of strident and unequivocal disavowal) without considering the relationship between those logics and those bodies who bear them is to risk aligning with the forces that would deny the fervor of black life, who would suggest that in order to become life at all it must become something other than black. And what it means to "consider the relationship" is to reveal something about, as Baldwin points us to, the *underside* of the stereotype, to think about what is held there, in the image we hate and reject yet continue to battle with and against. If "what it means to be a Negro in America can perhaps be suggested by an examination of the myths we perpetuate about [her],"[9] then we can afford neither to summarily dismiss nor to casually denigrate even an image as "objectionable" as the nappy-headed ho.

Ultimately, the repudiation of the nappy-headed ho during the Imus incident revealed the extent to which stereotype discourse goes hand in hand with what Lisa Marie Cacho calls "a politics of misrecognition."[10] In attending to the important distinction between stereotyping and criminalization as it relates to gang members, Cacho contends that "to be stereotyped as a criminal is to be misrecognized as someone who committed a crime, but to be criminalized is to be prevented from being law-abiding."[11] Thus what it means to disavow the criminal stereotype is to disavow being misrecognized as a criminal. In the case at hand, the nappy-headed ho is the articulation of a criminality, both formal and informal, from which the defenders of the Rutgers women sought to prevent them from being associated. But what I suggest in what follows is that by refusing to repudiate either criminality *or* the tradition of which Baldwin speaks, those who bear the mark of the nappy-headed ho gesture to a way of life that Bigger Thomas and those he stands in for completely forecloses.

THE UNDERSIDE

On May 30, 2006, Carmea Erving sat in a Peoria courtroom anxiously waiting for her opportunity to speak. Although, by her own admission, she is not particularly demonstrative and is not accustomed to speaking in public, she had spent the previous sleepless night preparing herself to confront the man who had admitted to murdering her mother less than two years earlier. She had committed to the public eulogy because she wanted to say something about the life Brenda Erving had lived, about the kind of mother she had been to her and her two younger sisters, about the kind of grandmother she had been to her grandchildren. She wanted to say something about her mother as an individual human being with likes and dislikes, with strengths and flaws, and whose unique presence mattered to the people in her life. She wanted to convey what had never been conveyed in the news coverage surrounding her mother's death and what could never be conveyed by the prosecutorial mechanisms used to bring Larry Bright, her mother's killer, to account for his crimes.[12]

It was an opportunity that never came. What did happen was that Bright entered a plea deal that spring day that allowed him to escape the death penalty in exchange for admitting to the murders of Brenda Erving and seven other black Peoria-area women—Shirley Ann Trapp, Laura Lollar, Linda Neal, Sabrina Payne, Shaconda Thomas, Tamara Walls, and Barbara Williams—and gave a twenty-five-word apology that came in the form of a letter read by his attorney.[13] And just like that, it was over. The promise made to Carmea by the prosecution that she would be able to speak for and about her mother was forgotten or forsaken, and the plea deal that she and other of her family members had never been comfortable or completely on board with was finalized. For all intents and purposes, the nightmare that had plagued Peoria's black community since the first dead body had been discovered in a cornfield in the summer of 2003 was over—the killer sent off to prison for the rest of his life, the victims' families left to grieve, to mourn, to pick up the pieces. But for Carmea the sense that she had been "played two times," first by the man who viciously took her mother's life and then by the prosecution that she felt never sufficiently considered her and her family's needs and wishes, continued to haunt her long after everyone— the court, the police, the lawyers, the reporters, the community—had moved on. And it is just this sort of haunting, this trace of the mother that lingers in the need to hold someone accountable for her stolen life (a life she made fugitive before the theft could occur) and that compels her daughter's attempt to bring her life close, that is the foundational grammar of black sociality.

In October 2013, almost nine years to the day after Brenda Erving was killed, I visited her daughter Carmea at her home in central Peoria. Although we are both Peorians who had grown up on the South Side (meaning we had, at most, one and a half degrees of separation between us) and had been in occasional communication since I'd first begun my research several years earlier, it was our first time meeting in person. She had agreed to talk to me in person and on camera, both so that I could have visual documentation of our conversation and because she felt it was past time that she tell the story that had been denied her years earlier. I'd welcomed her to invite her younger sisters, neither of whom I'd ever spoken with before, to the conversation as well. The middle sister, Tyrhonda, was there waiting with Carmea when I showed up, and we quickly realized that Tyrhonda and I had gone to the same grade school and middle school together at the same time, although we'd always run in different circles and had therefore never gotten to know each other before this meeting. The youngest sister was not there, and they did not give a reason for her absence. I did not ask for one.

We situated ourselves in the living room, a warmly appointed midsize room just off the kitchen in which a silent television played steadily in the background. Carmea and Tyrhonda sat closely together on a brown leather sofa, its back facing a stairwell that led upstairs. As I set up my equipment, the two sisters sat patiently waiting, talking very quietly or not at all; sometimes one or the other would gaze at the television, and sometimes they would both just look off into space. There was another person in the room, a young black man whose name I was told but whom I was never told anything else about, though I had the sense he was meant to be there as support for one or both of the women. Throughout the interview he sat just off camera looking at his phone, never looking up or speaking. Once we began talking, there remained a certain stillness in the room where we sat, yet all was not quiet. Carmea and Tyrhonda, both of whom were in in their midthirties at the time of our meeting, have between them seven children, and it was clear that some or all of them were nearby, being just barely contained somewhere beyond the kitchen. While Carmea informed me that she had prepared her children for my visit and had given them the "talking to" (you know the one, something to the effect of "You had better be on your best behavior while we have company . . . or else"), and thus I was only peripherally aware of their presence while we were talking, in the taped interview their adolescent chatter and noise making establish the background of our conversation.

For Carmea preparing her children for my visit was about more than simply getting their behavior in line, however. She told me, "Today was the first day I've *ever* had to explain anything to my kids." Of her two daughters the oldest was eleven at the time of our interview and was a toddler at the time of her grandmother's death, while her younger daughter, then seven, wasn't yet born. And so when they asked Carmea why I would be coming to their house, she told them that she was going to be talking with me about her mother's death and that her mother had been murdered. She explained what that meant to them as best she could, but, as children will do, the girls quickly turned their attention to other things. Carmea breathed a sigh of relief because it was a conversation she'd been dreading for some time, and she had steeled herself to respond to any and all questions they might ask. But beyond her oldest daughter's inquiry into just what a "serial killer" was, they did not probe too deeply. The situation was markedly different for Tyrhonda, whose children are the oldest of Brenda's grandchildren:

TYRHONDA: See, at the time—I have the oldest kids. So at the time, my kids—like my middle son, he's—he have, like, behavioral issues, he always have. My mom was the only person that could deal with this baby. Like, it's days I *cried* 'cause this baby was jus—he was a horrible child.

CARMEA: Don't talk about Taz.

TYRHONDA: And that's what my mama named him, Taz, 'cause she said he destroyed everything in his path. [*Laughter*] And this is why she lived with me on and off 'cause she had to get this baby. And people that knew my mom, they knew Taz. They hadn't never met him, but they knew Taz 'cause this is all she talked about. . . . My kids were older so they knew who my mom was, and like, my baby—it was the day before my baby's second birthday that they found my mom's body. So we were moving [to a new home] and preparing for my baby's birthday party. At the funeral, I'm holding my baby and walk to my mom casket. My baby reach for my mom to pick him up. So I'm just *done*. . . . My oldest son end up seeing a psychiatrist for a little while after it happened. Well, I ain't gonna say [a psychiatrist]—a "grief counselor."

Carmea remembers well the day she found out her mother was dead. She was at her job at a popular beauty supply store in town when her uncle called her "crying, crying, crying." He told her that Brenda was dead and that the police were at her grandmother's house, which was just a few minutes away from her job. She doesn't remember getting in her car or how she got there, but she does remember being at her grandmother's house and being approached by a police official, who told her "they had found her dead, on the side of a road, naked, with only socks on." After demanding proof that the body was actually that of her mother and being told she'd been identified through fingerprint analysis, Carmea then took off in a panic with their youngest sister and went looking for Tyrhonda, whom she wanted to tell directly so that she would not find out from the news or some other source. As it turned out, Tyrhonda was in the process of moving, and at that very same moment she was angrily driving around town looking for their mother because Brenda had agreed to help her look after her children while she moved and hadn't shown up. Eventually Carmea and their sister caught up with Tyrhonda at her home, and that is when they broke the news to her.

Brenda Erving was the last victim. Her body was discovered on October 15, 2004, and by December 2004 Larry Bright was in custody. He had been linked to one of the dead women, Linda Neal, through DNA evidence after several other women in the life, including another would-be murder victim of Bright's who had been able to get away from him, although not before being raped, provided identifying information.[14] The relative speed with which Bright was caught following Brenda's death was at least in part because it was not until then that the investigation into the women's deaths seemed to become a real priority for the police and that the community became actively involved en masse. For instance, it was not until September 27 of that year, less than a month before Brenda's death, that a ten-member task force made up of officials from Peoria County and neighboring Tazewell County, where two of the bodies had been found, was created to investigate what was at that time the unsolved deaths of five black women and the reported disappearances of three others.[15] Weeks later the task force was expanded to include fifteen members, a phone line for tips was established, and a $20,000 reward for information leading to the arrest and indictment of the killer was offered.[16] Additionally, the first of two town-hall meetings meant to keep residents abreast of the investigation was not held until October 25, ten days *after* the final body was discovered, when some five hundred people showed up to ask questions of the representative police departments. During the meeting tempers flared as residents questioned police about the slow pace of the investigation and its racial/racist implications—to which the police responded that they didn't see race as either an issue or a problem in the investigation, an argument they made throughout the duration of the case. The second town-hall meeting was held on November 8 and was attended by roughly four hundred residents but did not involve police or city officials.[17]

Despite the genuine outpouring of community support and local attention the case eventually received, Carmea and Tyrhonda were quick to note that the perception given in the media was often not on par with their actual experiences. They noted that two of the community leaders whose names come up time and again in relation to the case, and who became something of the media face of the community while it was ongoing, seemed to be concerned precisely with that, with, as Carmea put it, "using our story to kinda make them look like they were the bigger people of the community." The sisters had been told that money was being collected on their behalf to help with ongoing costs; but it never materialized, and they were never given a straight answer about where the funds were or how they had been spent. When they requested use of the church that one of the leaders pastored for their mother's funeral, they were told they would have to pay a fee because they were not members. And in what stood out as a particularly egregious moment for them, the leaders showed up at Bright's sentencing to "speak for the families" without ever having spoken to them or anyone else from their family. "How you gonna speak for me," they asked, "when you never spoke *to* me?"

Carmea and Tyrhonda were also troubled by the seeming lack of involvement of many of the family members of the other victims. Tyrhonda stated that whenever they would attend various hearings and court appearances associated with the case, other than the sentencing to which the aforementioned leaders put in a notable appearance, "it'd be just me and Mea. When, all these women this man killed, me and Mea be the only black face you see in the courtroom. Me and Mea." They felt as if many family members did not want to deal with the deaths and would have rather they just "left it alone," rather than continue to advocate on behalf of the women as they did right up until Bright was convicted and sentenced. Their attempts to connect with the other family members did not pan out for what they assumed was lack of interest, and while they were hoping to be involved in memorial services for the women whose bodies were never recovered because they had been burned to ash by Bright, memorial services for those women, from what they knew, had still never taken place. Although they could appreciate how difficult the losses were for the women's loved ones, they felt as if the families all would have gotten through it better if they had tried to work through it collectively, and they also wondered if more active family involvement earlier on could have changed the course of things, perhaps even resulted in fewer deaths. Further, they had the sense that at least part of what was at issue for the families was embarrassment, embarrassment at how the women lived their lives, embarrassment even at how they died. But

Carmea and Tyrhonda were very clear that although they never approved of Brenda's drug use and whatever she might have done to acquire those drugs, they were never at any point embarrassed by their mother. Instead, they tell the story of a woman who was, most importantly, *theirs*:

> TYRHONDA: If you ask anybody in the street that know my mom, they gonna know her from cooking chicken! . . .
> CARMEA: She end up even getting her own restaurant at a certain point.
> TYRHONDA: Selling chicken!
> TERRION: Which is amazing! . . . And how did she end up with her own restaurant?
> TYRHONDA: It was—somebody she was involved with, he was in the restaurant business.
> CARMEA: She had all the recipes and the secrets, and he had the financial part. So in order for her to give up the secrets, she wanted her own. And she got her own!
> TYRHONDA: She took it and ran! It did *very* well.
> TERRION: What was the name of it?
> TYRHONDA AND CARMEA: Chicken, Ribs, and More.[18]
> CARMEA: All she did, she cared about her grandkids. And cooking and babysitting. Like, whenever we needed her, she would be there. And she gonna cook, make some cornbread, all the goofy stuff grandparents would do. She would make 'em a pot of cornbread, like, who just want a pan of cornbread? Just feed the kids cornbread. They want it 'cause she put sugar in it! [*Laughter*] Mom, come on. All the kids hype off sweet cornbread!

It is this primary sociality, this way of being together that both precedes and exceeds the public sphere, that Brenda, Carmea, Tyrhonda, and other similarly situated black women have something to tell us about. It is a sociality encapsulated by the term *in the life*, which is sometimes used by women who are involved in prostitution to describe their "work" and who rarely use *prostitute, sex worker*, or any of their derivatives to define themselves but whose relevant self-descriptors, when they use any at all, tend to include words like *girls, hookers, hustlers, pros*, or *hos*.[19] As a term of art *in the life* is of no small consequence because there is, in my view, something profound, instructive, even moving about an ideological stance that establishes a space of vitality, a space for living, that is primarily inhabited by those who engage in activities that put them in close proximity to death and whose existence is externally conditioned by their supposed nonexistence. But to fully comprehend black social life is also to understand this external pressure and how it exerts itself within the delusory rubrics of value.

BLACKNESS AND VALUE

More than twenty-five years ago, in a now well-known speech delivered at the University of Michigan, Toni Morrison addressed the African American presence in American literature by way of *Moby-Dick*. She noted that Herman Melville's most famous text was a prominent exemplar of how canonical (read: white, male) American literature studiously grapples with, is actually seething with, blackness and black folks. This grappling does not announce itself, of course, but is instead concealed by what Hortense Spillers might call "layers of attenuated meanings."[20] Morrison suggests that the unspeakable thing that goes unspoken in *Moby-Dick* is not Melville's relationship to blackness or black people, or even his relationship to white people, but his relationship to whiteness itself. And she suggests that what Melville dared not speak was neither a disdain for slavery nor a charitable belief in the humanity of black folks but a concern over the very ideology of whiteness—whiteness as privilege, as superiority, as terror.[21]

Wherever we might land on the question of Melville and his kin and their racial or racist inclinations, what Morrison posits is the ever-present thereness of the unspoken and the invisible, or the un-visible. She is concerned, then, with "ghostly matters,"[22] with tracing the genealogy of structured absences that enable and are enabled by black sociality. Thus it is here, in the realm of the unspeakable unspoken, that I now linger. And because there is perhaps no one better suited to the task of dealing with what lingers than Morrison, it is at the end of her masterwork *Beloved* that I begin this particular inquiry.

> Everybody knew what she was called, but nobody anywhere knew her name. Disremembered and unaccounted for, she cannot be lost because no one is looking for her, and even if they were, how can they call her if they don't know her name? Although she has claim, she is not claimed. . . .
>
> It was not a story to pass on.

They forgot her like a bad dream. After they made up their tales, shaped and decorated them, those that saw her that day on the porch quickly and deliberately forgot her. It took longer for those who had spoken to her, lived with her, fallen in love with her, to forget, until they realized they couldn't remember or repeat a single thing she said, and began to believe that, other than what they themselves were thinking, she hadn't said anything at all. So, in the end they forgot her too. Remembering seemed unwise. . . .

It was not a story to pass on.

So they forgot her. Like an unpleasant dream during a troubling sleep. Occasionally, however, the rustle of a skirt hushes when they wake, and the knuckles brushing a cheek in sleep seem to belong to the sleeper. Sometimes the photograph of a close friend or relative—looked at too long—shifts, and something more familiar than the dear face itself moves there. They can touch it if they like, but don't, because they know things will never be the same if they do.

This is not a story to pass on.

Down by the stream in back of 124 her footprints come and go, come and go. They are so familiar. Should a child, an adult place his feet in them, they will fit. Take them out and they disappear again as though nobody ever walked there. By and by all trace is gone, and what is forgotten is not only the footprints but the water too and what is down there. The rest is weather. Not the break of the disremembered and unaccounted for, but wind in the eaves, or spring ice thawing too quickly. Just weather. Certainly no clamor for a kiss.

Beloved.[23]

What does it mean to name the avowedly disremembered and unaccounted for "Beloved"? What enables a story that is not to be passed on? What manner of forgetting presses in on our sleep, forces us to forget what is too hard to remember? How do we go about remembering when what is forgotten are not only the footprints but the water too and what is down there? This is a set of questions that not only matters in the realm of ghostly haunts or haints but reverberates across the terrain of black social life. In Morrison's exploration of American literature, she asks it this way: "Looking at the scope of American literature, I can't help thinking that the question should never have been 'Why am I, an Afro-American, absent from it?' It is not a particularly interesting query anyway. The spectacularly interesting question is, 'What intellectual feats had to be performed by the author or his critic to erase me from a society seething with my presence, and what effect has that performance had on the work?' What are the strategies of escape from knowledge? Of willful oblivion?"[24] So the question is not why but how. And what. I am not so concerned with asking why these black women's lives don't seem to matter to what we might call the, or a, public sphere. I'm not asking why the media does not pay any real attention when four, five, six, ten, fifteen black women are slaughtered right in a row or why so many activist groups and leaders don't respond to it as the utter dispossession that it is or why it takes four, five, six, ten, fifteen dead black women before the police will pay serious attention. I'm not asking these questions because we mostly know the answers to them. But, that said, the reason I'm not asking them is not because they aren't important but because they don't reach far enough, they don't stretch us enough, they don't challenge us enough. I'm not asking them because, as a diverse range of black cultural theorists have already suggested to us, questions about why "they don't treat us right" are too often predicated on a confounding, and often heavily class-inflected, discourse on rights and citizenship to which it's not completely clear these women ever actually belonged. One such theorist is a sixteen-year-old young woman referenced as Harriet Jones in John Langston Gwaltney's important ethnography *Drylongso*. Harriet is a project dweller whose mother is an alcoholic and whose ill-intentioned father passes into whiteness, and out of her life, as the opportunities arise. She is also an unmitigated "good girl" who finds solace in the flute and eighteenth-century English essays. In talking about her relationship to America, this is what Harriet has to say:

> We keep doing all the things America stands for, and the better Americans we are, the bigger suckers we are. But we are doing what we think we should do, not what white people say we should do, but I still feel like a sucker. . . . All through history, I think, it has been like that. Lincoln freed the slaves because he had to do that, but Harriet Tubman freed them by risking her own personal life because she knew that it was the right thing to do. Sometimes I wonder if there are any other Americans besides us. . . . I think it is a kind of suicide to like anything that hates you. If we are the only people who really want to be Americans, what

is the point? I don't mean jumping up and down on certain days and making a lot of noise, but doing what everybody knows is right and not doing things you know have got to be wrong.[25]

For Harriet what it means to be an American is not tied up in things like birthright or rote patriotism but in how people treat each other. And so she puts exceptionalism to the test, finds it lacking, and wonders if black people aren't the only Americans. If we take Harriet's insight as a serious intellectual inquiry into "why repudiating criminality and recuperating social value so often reproduce the problems we mean to resolve,"[26] then we can begin to see how struggles over and demands for normative inclusion and equal rights cannot do the work that needs to be done. They cannot make everything all right. They aren't even suited to the task.

Accordingly, what Brenda Erving and similarly situated women gesture toward is an alternative mode of black sociality or, to lift terms from Stefano Harney and Fred Moten, an undercommon unit of study that cannot be contained in or by terms like *American* or *citizen*.[27] It is the recognition of a right of refusal, a right to refuse that which has been previously refused to you. This confrontation occurs in *Beloved* at the moment Sethe commits the ultimate violation in the name of what Morrison calls the "necessity of freedom."[28] By killing her beloved rather than yield to her return to bondage, Sethe refuses, outright rejects, the law that will not acknowledge her or her offspring as anything more than chattel. Thus the terror that animates the text is not that Sethe murders her baby girl but the conditions that enabled that heinous choice and the continued resonances of those conditions into the present.

When Paul D arrives on Sethe's porch in the opening pages of *Beloved*, one of the first questions he asks is about the death of Sethe's mother-in-law, Baby Suggs. "Was it hard?" he asks. "I hope she didn't die hard." "Soft as cream," Sethe replies. "Being alive was the hard part."[29] If we trace the line from Baby Suggs to Brenda Erving through Sethe and Beloved and the multitude of untold others, fictional and not, and we assume that "being alive was the hard part," it might occasion a way of thinking about the addictions that frequented Brenda and so many others who share her fate as something more than annihilation or self-hate or self-medication or any of the other terms that get used in the service of pathologizing the addict. It might help us to at least consider the possibility of addiction as refusal, as a fugitive existence that is "separate from the logical, logistical, the housed and the positioned."[30] It is to say, "being alive is the hard part," but because I want to stay alive, I have to flee into something that may kill me.

Here, then, is the unspeakable thing—not just the possibility that one could be kept alive by the same thing that is killing you but that this fragile positionality beckons toward another kind of space, a space in which invisibility has a certain kind of purchase. If Avery Gordon is right that "hypervisibility is a persistent alibi for the mechanisms that render one *un*-visible," then women in the life are among both the most visible and most un-visible of subjects.[31] And it is from this location that they subvert the rubrics of exchange that would consign them either to the realm of the valued or to the realm of the devalued. Here, where they go unseen and unknown, they have knowledge of the invaluable, the outside of value, a wild that consumption dares not enter. In this space value is radically invalidated, and what it means to be beloved is harnessed neither to notions of righteousness or esteem, respectability or veneration, nor to any of the ontological configurations these terms would attempt to call into alignment. The reason these women, these seemingly discarded, un-visible, black women matter is not just because they are among a long line of discarded un-visible peoples, black or otherwise, women or otherwise, whom we need to feel bad for or about but because even as they are *on* the market, they are not *of* the market, because even in their discardedness they lay claim to an elusive way of being that is *in the life*, and what it means to be in the life has significant implications for blackness, black studies, black folks—and beyond.

In *Blackness and Value*, Lindon Barrett is concerned, as I am here, with thinking about the anatomization of value and the forms of sociality it inaugurates or lays bare. He argues that value is inherently structured by violence and that said violence is obscured by the very thing it produces, which is not simply value but the establishment of *binaries* of value, including whiteness and blackness, the valued and the devalued. Value thus has a twofold structure wherein "value as force" produces "value as form," which is then represented by the binaries of value therein created. Barrett recognizes that "the valorizing process, which is to say the formalizing of value, the instatement of the valued, relies in the first place upon violence as well as on the conversion of that violence into novel significance, into a renewed recognition of a privileged form."[32] Later he reveals how this "conversion of violence" occurs in both its physical and its immaterial forms via the black female body, arguing that it is the figure of the whore that most clearly delineates the conditionality of black women in the United States and that there is a direct relation between the whore as sign and the slave, that is, that other market-based figure of black degradation:

> In point of fact, however, conceptual and legal proscriptions against the conflation of the market and the familial (which ought to subsume the erotic entirely in strictly controlled ways) are never wholly unqualified. Gayle Rubin, for example, points out that when one considers matters closely one recognizes that "[s]ex law incorporates a very strong prohibition against mixing sex and money" with one crucial exception, which is "via marriage." The seeming opposition between the familial and the market is ultimately spurious. Thus, to position black female bodies historically and legally as the exclusive site at which these proscriptions do not obtain, rather than acknowledging this point of fact, amounts to incorporating by law and custom black female bodies as the paramount site at which sexuality is routinely and perversely commodified in monetary terms and money routinely (and with equal perversion) accounted in sexual terms. African American female bodies are thus established as what might be understood as the ur-site of "prostitution," a site of both social and natural pollution. As it is with the body/person who is a slave, the body/person who is a prostitute is in some ways indistinguishable from the structures of the market. This identity is inscribed for the slave in terms of one's relation to one's labor and for the prostitute in terms of what is imagined as one's most intimate relation to one's body.[33]

Barrett demonstrates the consequence of this form of violent subjectification by way of a reading of Lutie Johnson, the protagonist of Ann Petry's 1946 novel *The Street*. The novel opens with Lutie, who is estranged from her adulterous husband, determinedly looking for an apartment to rent on 116th Street in Harlem, where she resigns herself to living until she is able to provide something "better" for herself and her eight-year-old son. She is consumed with the sense that 116th Street is a place to get away from, a place where black boys like her son are conditioned to "sweep floors and mop stairs the rest of their lives."[34] Lutie, Barrett argues, is also in a relentless struggle against the conscriptions of the oppressive sign of the whore. Sensing that she is always already read in terms of her purported physical availability and sexual proclivities, the "highly respectable, married, mother of a small boy" actively resists the advances of her landlord, Jones, who eventually attempts to rape her; Mrs. Hedges, a tenant in her building who runs a brothel and is initially looking to recruit Lutie; and a band leader named Boots Smith, who offers her a singing gig that turns out to be an unpaid position meant to lure Lutie into the bed of Junto, the white man who owns the casino where Boots works.[35] By the novel's climactic end, when Boots attempts to take Lutie, sexually, for himself before passing her along to Junto, Lutie's frustration at the conditions of her (im)possibility as a married-but-single impoverished black woman with only her perceived sexual favors to use as leverage against her circumstances overwhelms her, and in a fit of rage she viciously bludgeons Boots to death with an iron candlestick. Immediately thereafter she flees Harlem for Chicago, purchasing a one-way train ticket and leaving her young son behind. Of this Barrett contends that "Lutie's act of scripting herself without this sign [of the whore], in her most violent effort to resist its imagined legitimacy, turns out to be the very act that forever scripts her outside the bounds of the all-American suburb."[36] Put differently, Lutie's attempt to assert her value *within the parameters established by value* ultimately consigns her to the state of the utterly devalued, in word and in deed.

Both the fictional story of Lutie Johnson and the real-life terror of black women in the life expose the perversions of a value system engendered by violence. In the case of the latter this engendering is made evident by the fact that, at least in the public sphere where grievability is hotly contested, whatever normative value they do incur comes only after their vicious and untimely deaths. In short, they reveal most urgently that "violence . . . is the opening that allows value."[37] But while Lutie's story suggests the consequences of an investment in this system taken to its extreme end, black women in the life suggest what it might mean to resist, or "dismember," normative valuation altogether.[38] Whereas Lutie's attempt to align herself against the figure of the whore implicates her within the very mechanisms that produce that figure, women in the life, as its most literal embodiment, are, ironically, at a remove from it.

What I mean to suggest, in other words, is that by subverting the mandates of normative, acceptable female behavior—which, as Carmea and Tyrhonda remind us, does not mean they do not *mother*—and forcing us to grapple with the indices of non-value, women in the life both resist and call attention to the violence that conditions their lives. They reveal to us that what it means to be in the life is to be part of a fugitive, intramural sociality that reveals, even revels in, the underside of the stereotype—or that which is foreclosed by the scandal of representation—while simultaneously resisting the dichotomies of value that structure the dominant social order. Importantly, "black people who experience or act on same-sexual desire" also often refer to themselves as being in the life in addition to or in lieu of other terms used to mark sexual identity.[39] This is an important correlation not because I want to suggest that everyone in this latter group necessarily adheres to the protocols I am attempting to delimit by my use of the term *in the life* but because this simultaneous use of the term helps to reveal both how the valences of value are structured by heteronormativity and how vulnerable black populations go about claiming their space in the world. What we might subsequently conclude, then, is that those who are in the life are in the best position to help us reckon with heteronormative privilege, nonnormative heterosexuality, and "the ways in which heteronormativity works to support and reinforce institutional racism, patriarchy, and class exploitation."[40] Put differently, "examining how 'value' and its normative criteria are naturalized and universalized enables us to uncover and unsettle the heteropatriarchal, legal, and neoliberal investments that dominant and oppositional discourses share in rendering the value of nonnormativity illegible."[41] In short, to be in the life is to have a special angle of vision on the illogics of value and to bear a critical posture toward its enabling conditions.

WHAT PLAYS IN PEORIA

In May 2014 the first "Recognize Richard" fund-raiser was held in Peoria. The impetus for the event was to assist in raising the $100,000 needed to complete the casting of a nine-foot-tall memorial statue of Peoria-born comedian Richard Pryor that was first idealized by local artist Preston Jackson more than ten years earlier. When the statue was finally erected a year later, it became the first major recognition of Pryor by a city that has been slow at best in paying homage to one of its best-known and most culturally significant native sons.[42] Those in the know suggest that the lack of attention paid to Pryor by Peoria over the years has had as much or more to do with his less-than-reputable lifestyle and public persona as it has with his risqué, profanity-laced brand of comedy-cum-social commentary.[43] Add to this the fact that Pryor depicted Peoria as a model city only insofar as it "had the niggers under control," where his early life was conditioned by the brothel he was raised in by his grandmother, and where he first became acquainted with the illicit pleasures that notoriously frequented his adult life, and it perhaps comes as no surprise that, regardless of whatever national acclaim he received over his lifetime and his now-doubtless legacy, Richard Pryor, Superstar, has been difficult for a city that has historically posited itself as emblematic of "Anytown, USA" to reconcile with its image of itself.[44]

Pryor the Peorian. When I tell people of a certain age that I am from Peoria, they almost inevitably mention that it was the birthplace of Richard Pryor. They know this one thing about my hometown if they know nothing else substantive about it (and quite often they do not). Despite the understandable frustration some residents have had with Peoria's failure to recognize Pryor, it is this "failure" that is, I submit, Pryor's truest legacy. The fact that Peoria has become synonymous with Pryor despite and in the face of Peoria's disavowal of him suggests that this "failure" is not one at all, at least not in the terms that were essential to Pryor himself. Or, to put it another way, *there is no failure in the life*. Pryor *embodied* Peoria, and he carried the place that he, Brenda, Tyrhonda, Carmea, and myself knew and know with him and used it and its people as evidence of a thriving black sociality that he never attempted to hold himself apart from, even as he mocked and critiqued it.

In an interview Pryor gave in 1974, he was asked what he thought about the claims some white people were making that he was racist because he usually portrayed them as bigoted and ignorant. Pryor responded, "Good. I'm glad that's a concern now all of a sudden. Maybe they'll burn up *Gone with the Wind*." He went on to say, "I don't care what they think. They don't have to come see me. Ain't no niggas ever said to me, 'I think you're racist because you're portraying white folks so funny.'"[45] What I would submit is that it was not his profanity or drug abuse or abuse of women that ultimately made Pryor so unsettling for our hometown and all those whom it stands in for but this: his wholesale preoccupation with black folks, what black folks thought, how black folks lived, and his utter refusal of and critical posture toward constraint. Accordingly, what Pryor gestures toward is a way of life, of social life, that bears an antagonistic relationship to the violence out of which it emerges and to which it sometimes succumbs. He, like all those in the life, inherently understood the possibilities of the extralegal, the amoral, the improper, the uncontained, and the dislocated.

One of Pryor's now-numerous biographers once said of him that "whatever his topic, he spoke the unspeakable."[46] No doubt his ability to speak those things that went unspoken had to do with his relationship to the people and places from which he came. When talking about his relationship with the actor Billy Dee Williams, whom he described as being so consummately aware of his image that he would not be seen in public with him and his friend and fellow comedian Paul Mooney for fear that they would somehow tarnish him, Pryor said, "I didn't remotely identify with that worrywart shit. My life was populated by characters. There was Prophet, a moody but talented painter. Dirty Dick. A whole circus of hustlers, whores, winos, and hangers-on. I thought they were people who knew stuff worth knowing."[47]

It seems to me that the "stuff" Brenda Erving and other similarly situated women know that's worth knowing is something those folks who are so concerned with tarnishing their image that they can't be bothered with them do not know. And that is that there is something to be said for living outside of value, for acknowledging the absolute violence of value, of being party to a system in which one either has value or is devalued and consequently must make all sorts of diabolical concessions, alignments, and, ultimately, misalignments in order to stay on the positive end of that scale. So the call here is not a simple request for visibility. It is not just a matter of calling the media or the police or the community organizations to task for their failures. It is not even about trying to valiantly assert the value of these women's lives. Avery Gordon tells us that ghosts haunt us not just because they want us to return to the past but because they want us to reckon with the repression of the past in the present.[48] This, ultimately, is about a reckoning. It is about bringing close the lives of those who are not simply "other" but who are fundamentally *us* and who have so much to tell us not just about who we are but also about who we can be.

It is a story we must pass on.

AFTERWORD

We Gon' Be Alright

While I was in the final stages of writing this book, I returned home to Peoria because my mother was to undergo a major surgery. Because of the extended recovery time the surgery required, I decided to look into having a housecleaning service attend to my parents' home once a week for the duration of her recovery. After several attempted phone inquiries I finally reached a company that was potentially willing to do the job, but before they would agree to it, I was informed they would need to send a manager out to do a site inspection to ensure it would be "safe" given that my parents live on the south (read: black) end of town. The manager, a woman of color, assured me upon her arrival that her visit should not be taken as an offense but that she just had to be careful when sending her employees to the area (something that clearly did not happen with any frequency and reflects my own relative privilege). Although I was indeed offended, because my time was limited and I was unable to find anyone else, I went ahead and hired the service after passing the "inspection," which essentially amounted to some sort of vague assessment by the manager that my parents lived in a safe-enough place (I suppose because there were no drive-by shootings or gangsters sitting on the front stoop or drug dealers standing on the corner). I did not initially tell my mother about the manager's comments, but I had to return to Michigan, where I was living at the time, before the first cleaning took place; and when I called her to inquire about how it had gone, she told me that the young black woman who had been sent to do the cleaning (who, incidentally, had grown up in the area and gone to school with my little brother) had told her that although they "didn't mean to be racist," certain people at the company had asked her if she wouldn't mind cleaning my parents' home because the rest of the cleaning staff was "uncomfortable" going, as we say, "down the hill."

My compatriots at the World Foot Locker on the West Side of Chicago where I worked throughout my college years would have been proud.[1] For four years they heckled me for being from a place (none of them had ever been to) where, allegedly, crime was nonexistent, all our gangsters were "fake," and our primary form of entertainment was, naturally, cow tipping and the occasional tractor-pull. In an environment in which almost all of the employees were black or brown and came from some of the most notorious neighborhoods of Chicago's West and South Sides—with the notable exception of the head store manager, who was always white and male no matter who actually filled the position—I was something of an anomaly. My protestations that I was raised in the blackest part of my town and that I was also from the hood, that I had also known people who had been sent to prison for drug or gang activity or had been shot to death (an admittedly bizarre, but ultimately telling, thing to be competing over), were of absolutely no consequence. It probably didn't help that I was a full-time college student at a major university (when for many of them selling shoes was *their* full-time gig even if, as a number of them did, they attended city college on the side) or that my parentally cultivated churchgirlism still clung to me like a second skin.

After hearing the "not racist" comments about how dangerous and frightening the place where my family had lived since I was in fourth grade without so much as a rock through the window supposedly was, and after being reminded by my mother about the things she continues to hear everyone from pizza delivery people to local politicians allege about the deprivations of life down the hill, I could not help but reflect on the irony of my attempts at debating my hood cred with my Foot Locker friends those many years ago. And they were, most assuredly, my friends. Other than the time I spent sleeping in my dorm room, I easily spent more time in that shoe store than I did on campus, and actually, the clowning of me and my gangster-deprived hometown by my coworker friends was *nothing* in comparison to how they talked about each other. Between trips to the back to grab shoes for customers, when foot traffic was light and we were just standing around the sales floor, as we were lounging around the break room, during transactions on busy weekend afternoons, after the gates went down at night and we were counting money, tagging shoes, sweeping floors, and refilling displays, they, basically, rhetorically annihilated each other (note: our customers were not immune from random but stealthy verbal attack either). You learned very quickly that if you were going to last there, not only did you have to be willing to work long hours on your feet, be competitive enough to outsell the next person, and be wily enough to deal with customers who would as soon curse you out as purchase your product, but you also had to take yourself very lightly, grow a thick skin, or be prepared to get your comedic skills up exponentially. And although it was a heavily male-dominated space, plenty of the women employed during my time there were industrious enough, mean enough, homegirl enough, or whatever-it-took enough to go toe-to-toe with the guys, both on and off the sales floor.

For a long time I thought what was most important about my college years was college itself, that because of my time there I was exposed to "the life of the mind" and consequently set on my current career path (after a minor detour through law school, where I quickly learned that becoming Clair Huxtable was not, in fact, a sensible life goal). What I know now is that the time I spent in class was both peripheral to and in alignment with the time I spent outside of class, particularly at my job but also at my Chicago church home, where my pastor was the first to help me consider that God damned America's treatment of me over and above any of the relatively minor biblical infractions I'd been previously convinced would doom me to a life of, or worse yet, *in* hell. Moreover, despite my wide-eyed exposure to the black intelligentsia—many of whom had overwhelmed me with their brilliance—the single most significant thing I learned while, but not solely because, I was a college student was the extension of something I had already learned in other places with other, usually much less formally educated people. And that is, I became more deeply aware of and committed to the process of being with and for black people.

This, I think, is no minor thing. In one of the last interviews James Baldwin gave before his death in 1987, he talked about the "irreducible injustice" of his position as a black writer who is *claimed* by black people. When asked whether he resented his position vis-à-vis the masses, Baldwin asserted that "someone who is not white and attempts to be in some way responsible is going to be claimed by multitudes of black kids. Just or unjust is irrelevant."[2] He went on to say, "I didn't resent it because it was an obligation that was impossible to fulfill. They have made you, produced you—and they have done so precisely so they could claim you. They can treat you very badly sometimes, as has happened to me. Still, they produced you because they need you and, for me, there's no way around that. Now, in order for me to execute what I see as my responsibility, I may have to offend them all, but that also comes with the territory. I don't see how I can repudiate it."[3] When I talk about what it means to be with and for black people, I mean neither to rehearse the rhetoric of solidarity nor to essentialize the meaning of blackness but to extend Baldwin's notion of the impossible obligation of black circumstance beyond the writer or the celebrity or the dubious "race man" in order to suggest that such an obligation is the very enabling condition of black social life. This is to say, "we're all in this together" is not simply empty rhetoric but the consummate description of black life. This is born out in our shared history, in our prolonged attentiveness to representative constructs, in the expression of our cultural forms and traditions, and in our collective devotedness to ensuring black lives matter. Baldwin reminds us that this is not always a happy condition, that the constraints of our togetherness can and sometimes do frustrate us and cause us pain. But what I have tried to suggest throughout *Scandalize My Name*—what I have learned from my grandmother and mother, the South Side of Peoria, and my Foot Locker friends as much as anyone or anyplace else—is that while blackness might be, as Frank Wilderson and others have informed us, predicated on death and violence, black social life is fundamentally irreducible to the terror that calls it into existence.

I'm well aware that the position I've taken throughout this text might be accused of "romanticizing," in particular, poor and working-class black people. My, perhaps unsatisfying, response to that charge is this: my experience of writing this book has been bookended by death. It began while I was in graduate school, and I was trying to grapple with the serial deaths of more than eight black women that had occurred in my hometown to virtually no outside attention whatsoever. Then, as I was completing the first draft of my manuscript in September 2013, KeiAmber Beard, one of the women who took part in the bachelorette party I discuss in the opening of chapter 3, was killed. At the age of twenty-four and pregnant with her first child, KeiAmber was shot to death in the middle of the night while lying next to James Irby, her twenty-nine-year-old partner, the supposed target, who was also shot and killed and whose ten- and seven-year-old children were listening in a nearby bedroom during the attack.[4] They lived on the

South Side of Peoria, not too far from the home where I grew up and where my parents continue to reside. In between these events, I lost my beloved grandmother, a friend from my Chicago church home succumbed to her battle with cancer, and my friend and former lover, a Los Angeles–based musician and Peoria native, died unexpectedly the night before my thirty-first birthday.

How to talk about these people, all of whom I came to know far outside the middle-class academic enclave I now inhabit, and the meaning of their lives and their deaths, not just for me and all the other people who knew and loved them but for *all* of us, black and otherwise, who are concerned about the social conditions of blackness and how those conditions shape and are shaped by the machinations of the U.S. apparatus? I could, of course, attempt to outline every racist, classist, sexist, heterosexist, toxic, debilitating, harmful thing that has ever happened in the lives of poor and working-class black folks (many of which, quite clearly, are also experienced by middle-class black people, even if the impact often differs). I could indict every organization, institution, and structure responsible for the existence of a socio-economic "bottom" and the situatedness of my subjects within it. But while I have endeavored to provide the necessary context for understanding the lives of those whom I discuss in these pages, I have also attempted to discuss their lives in their *fullness* which, at least from what I've been able to tell, is far more significant to *them* than solely delimiting the ill conditions of their existence. In my own experience of my natal community and all the other places like it where I have lived and traveled, black folks know full well that they live in and through some conspicuously bad shit. But what they also seem to know is how, as my fellow Peorian Richard Pryor would put it, to "keep some sunshine on their face."[5] Besides, as it turns out, *romance* is not a four-letter word.

ACKNOWLEDGMENTS

This is an intensely personal book, and there have been many people who have helped to nourish me through the writing process emotionally, intellectually, and otherwise. No person has been more important in this regard than my mother, Kim Crushshon Nelson, who, along with my late grandmother Bernice Turner, is the inspiration for this book. She and the rest of my "parental unit"—Perrion "Lump" Williamson, Mary Ann Williamson, and Rufus Nelson, Sr.—have sustained me with their unwavering love, support, and belief in me. Every good thing I am I owe to them.

I am fortunate to have a host of other family members who have supported me along this journey as well. In particular, I want to thank my siblings, Rufus Nelson, Jr., Tina Nelson Jackson, Bridgette Byrd, Teresa Allen, Carolyn Nunn, and Angela Morris, and all my brothers-in-law, nieces, and nephews for how they have modeled unconditional love for me. I must also thank my grandmother Owen Nelson, whose wisdom is a stabilizing force in my family, and my aunt Casandra "Sweet" Williamson and her daughters, Aftyn Branch and Alyssa Branch, who opened their home to me for a year while I was in graduate school. The time we spent together during that laughter-filled year, and have spent together since, informs so much of what I do. There are far too many of them to name here individually, but much love and many thanks also go out to the other members of the Williamson, Collier, and Nelson families for the many ways that they continue to enrich my life.

I was a graduate student in American studies and ethnicity at the University of Southern California when I first began doing the work that led me to this project, and I owe a special debt of gratitude to the intellectually formidable members of my doctoral committee who have been so instrumental in shaping my scholarly trajectory. I could not have asked for a more generous or capable adviser than Kara Keeling, a fellow Peorian, who has continued to encourage and support me from afar. Jack Halberstam and Ange-Marie Hancock provided invaluable guidance and feedback that still shapes and informs my thinking. Herman Gray has been a mentor of the highest order. His expertise, which he is always so gracious in sharing, and careful attention to my work have helped make me a much more rigorous and savvy scholar. Although circumstances prevented us from crossing the finish line together, Judith Jackson Fossett played a crucial role in both my intellectual growth and professional development, for which I am eternally grateful. Last but not least, there is no single person working in an academic institution anywhere who has made more of an impact on my life's work than Fred Moten. I met Fred during the very early days of my graduate school career, and of the innumerable things he's done over the ensuing years that I have to thank him for, none is more important than the belief he instilled in me that I have something important to say. I would not be the *person* I am today had he not taken the time to help me get "back to living again." It is a debt I can never repay.

I am also grateful to a number of other scholars who have modeled the sort of scholarship I aspire to and have, in ways large and small, acted as guides and helped to calibrate my thinking throughout this project, including Robin Kelley, Francille Rusan Wilson, Dorinne Kondo, Daria Roithmayr, Ruth Wilson Gilmore, Daphne Brooks, Nicole Fleetwood, Ula Taylor, Tavia Nyong'o, Candice Jenkins, and Margareth Etienne. Many years ago as an undergraduate student in African American studies at the University of Illinois at Chicago, I had the sheer good fortune of being under the tutelage of a cohort of brilliant professors who sparked and cultivated my initial interest in becoming a black studies scholar, and so I would be remiss if I did not thank them here: Dwight McBride, Barbara Ransby, Sharon Holland, Duriel Harris, Sterling Plumpp, and James Hall.

This book could not have been completed without the generous financial support of the Ford Foundation, which granted me fellowship funding at both the dissertation and postdoctoral levels; the American Association of University Women; and the College of Arts and Letters at Michigan State University. I must also express my gratitude to all of the individuals at the American Literatures Initiative and Fordham University Press who were so instrumental to this book's production. Chief among these was Helen Tartar, whose untimely death prevented her from seeing this book to completion but whose passionate dedication both to my work and to her craft first convinced me that Fordham was the ideal home for my work. In the tradition of Helen, my editor, Richard Morrison, served to be a generous and committed advocate whose advice and direction were invaluable to this process. I am also deeply grateful to the other members of the editorial and production staff at Fordham, as well as my reviewers, who, rather than attempt to wrangle this project into something else, provided me the critical support and encouragement necessary to make what it was better. Chapter 4 was previously published in modified form in *Social Text* 33, no. 1 (March 2015). Chapter 5 appears in modified form in *CR: The New Centennial Review* (forthcoming). I am thankful to Duke University Press and Michigan State University Press, respectively, for permission to reprint.

I wrote the bulk of this book while a faculty member at Michigan State University, and my research and teaching have been deeply enriched by the advice, support, and friendship of the exceptional colleagues I had the privilege of working with during my time there, including Sheila Contreras, Ellen McCallum, LaShawn Harris, Pero Dagbovie, Terah Chambers, Glenn Chambers, Lisa Biggs, Rae Paris, Django Paris, Yomaira Figueroa, Tacuma Peters, Tamara Butler, Chezare Warren, April Baker-Bell, David Kirkland, Kristie Dotson, Ken Harrow, Jessica Johnson, Zarena Aslami, Pat O'Donnell, David Stowe, Steve Arch, David Bering-Porter, Justus Nieland, Scott Michaelsen, and Linda Cornish.

While at MSU, I also benefited from the diligent and insightful assistance of Kristin Rowe, Briona Jones, and Tamika Keene, graduate students who are all well on their way to leaving their own institutional and intellectual footprints, as well as Wanda Jones, who as a law student provided invaluable research on my serial murder project. I am also grateful to a number of other graduate and undergraduate students at MSU who, even when they didn't realize they were doing so, helped me to think through the ideas presented here, particularly the terrifically smart and engaging students who were enrolled in the "Gender, Sexuality, and Black Feminist Thought" course I was teaching as I was completing my final revisions.

Speaking of students, one of the things I have learned at this point in my career that I try to impart to them is the absolute necessity of having nurturing space outside of the academic institutions where we labor. I was fortunate to find this space among a small group of fiercely devoted members at St. Stephens Community Church. They along with my pastor, Rev. Sameerah Shareef, took me in and, just as they were supposed to, put me to work almost as soon as I stepped through the doors. I must also acknowledge in this regard my phenomenal line dancing group, whose spirit of fun and camaraderie, and loving acceptance of my abundant miscues and misdirections, was the best possible of therapies.

I owe a very special debt of gratitude to two people who, from my very first days in East Lansing, extended a welcome to me that, despite my attempts, could never be overstayed. Tama Hamilton-Wray and Jeff Wray embraced me, not just as a colleague or as a fellow congregant but as part of their family. They kept me fed, kept me laughing, kept me from being lonely, and ultimately, kept me going when I needed it most. I must also thank their children, Jasmine, Kimani, and Elijah, for being so generous with their parents, their home, and their friendship, as well as Gwen Murray and Taylor McGhee, who so lovingly round out this extended family I have taken as my own.

I am grateful beyond measure for Constance Williams, Clarice Jones, and Timony Criss-Kirkwood, my homegirls in the truest sense of the word. I cannot imagine life without them and their families, which I also count as my own. Thank you for loving me through my flaws and grounding me where I need it most. A number of other special individuals have also sustained and enriched me, and by extension my work, by way of their presence in my life, including Crystal Bolden, Jeanine Cook, Deon Wright, Anitra Daugherty, Nina Daugherty, Kevin Gordon, Crystal Scott, Paul Techo, and the late Kowan Paul, whose loss is still deeply felt. Your friendship has made all the difference.

In the years since I first began graduate school, I have benefited tremendously from the support and friendship of a number of superdope intellectuals who have had a profound impact on my life, as well as my scholarship. No one has been more essential in this regard than Michelle Commander, whose loving kindness and generosity of spirit have sustained me through the best and worst of times. My brilliant brother-from-another-mother Ashon Crawley is a true inspiration, and our ongoing conversation is the soundtrack that plays every time I sit down to write. The special friendships I share with Lanita Jacobs, Imani Johnson, Aisha Finch, and Sharon Luk have fortified me immeasurably. I cannot imagine having made it this far along the journey without their good humor, warm embraces, meandering conversations, and critical insights to help light the way. I am also fortunate to count Laura Harris, Mark Padoongpatt, Crizella Wallace, Gretel Vera-Rosas, and Tamura Lomax among the comrades who have generously supported and sustained me over the years.

I am forever grateful to Rev. Jeremiah Wright, Jr., for all of the wisdom and guidance, spiritual and otherwise, he has so generously imparted to me over the years and for modeling the true meaning of a commitment to social justice. I am also deeply appreciative of LaToya Ruby Frazier for generously granting me permission to use her work on this book's cover and for her ongoing commitment to expressing, visually, the fullness of black life.

This book would not exist but for my experiences growing up on the South Side of Peoria, Illinois. Despite the ill things people often have to say about such places, I am tremendously grateful for being from a community of hardworking, deep-loving, straight-talking black folks, many of whom I have already thanked here, who have taught me just what it means to be with and for black people. I also want to thank Carmea Erving, Tyrhonda Erving, and the rest of the Erving family for their courage and for trusting me with the story of their beloved that is so essential to this book's central narrative, and Pam Adams, whose unselfish commitment to the cause was so instrumental in helping me to get my work off the ground. You are among the many reasons I am so proud to call Peoria home.

NOTES

INTRODUCTION

1. Ralph Ellison, *Shadow and Act*, in *The Collected Essays of Ralph Ellison*, ed. John F. Callahan (New York: Modern Library, 2003), 58 (emphasis mine).

2. Rita Dove, "The House That Jill Built," in *Life Notes: Personal Writings by Contemporary Black Women*, ed. Patricia Bell-Scott (New York: Norton, 1994), 169.

3. In 1999 my grandmother wrote *A Brief Autobiography of Bernice L. Turner*, which outlines some of what I discuss here. She gave copies of the typed eleven-page document to several members of our family, including my mother and me.

4. Patricia Hill Collins, *Black Feminist Thought: Knowledge, Consciousness, and the Politics of Empowerment*, 2nd ed. (New York: Routledge, 2000), 16–17.

5. Ibid., 29–33.

6. Combahee River Collective, "The Combahee River Collective Statement," in *Home Girls: A Black Feminist Anthology*, ed. Barbara Smith (New Brunswick, NJ: Rutgers University Press, 2000), 264.

7. Robin D. G. Kelley, *Race Rebels: Culture, Politics, and the Black Working Class* (New York: Free Press, 1994), 8.

8. Hortense Spillers, interview by Tim Haslett, February 4, 1998, http://www.blackculturalstudies.org/spillers/spillers_intvw.html (site discontinued).

9. Kerry Washington, interview by Oprah Winfrey, *Oprah's Next Chapter*, OWN, December 9, 2012.

10. Olivia Pope's character is based on the real life of Judy Smith, a former deputy press secretary for President George H. W. Bush and owner of a Washington, D.C.-based crisis management firm.

11. For a discussion of representations of the black bourgeoisie and the terms by which the black middle-class has come to be known, see Vershawn Ashanti Young with Bridget Harris Tsemo, *From Bourgeois to Boojie: Black Middle-Class Performances* (Detroit: Wayne State University Press, 2011).

12. Lucille Clifton, "won't you celebrate with me," in *The Book of Light* (Port Townsend, WA: Port Canyon, 1993), 25.

13. Ralph Ellison, "That Same Pain, That Same Pleasure: An Interview," in *Shadow and Act*, 80, 76.

14. Ibid., 66–67.

15. Ibid., 68, 77–78.

16. Ibid., 80.

17. In recent years the term "ratchet" has come to signify similarly to "ghetto," although some of my students have informed me that "ratchet" has certain nuances of meaning and doesn't necessarily mean the same thing as "ghetto" in every instance. For a brief discussion of the history of the term, see Tamara Palmer, "Who You Calling Ratchet?," The Root, October 16, 2012.

18. David Wellman, "Reconfiguring the Color Line: Racializing Inner-City Youth and Rearticulating Class Hierarchy in Black America," *Transforming Anthropology* 17, no. 2 (2009): 134, doi: 10.1111/j.1548-7466.2009.01050.x.

19. Ibid., 134–35.

20. Ibid., 139.

21. John L. Jackson, Jr., *Real Black: Adventures in Racial Sincerity* (Chicago: University of Chicago Press, 2005), 59.

22. Kobena Mercer, *Welcome to the Jungle: New Positions in Black Cultural Studies* (New York: Routledge, 1994), 97.

23. For discussions of the contemporary natural hair movement see, for instance, Ruth La Ferla, "The Afro as a Natural Expression of Self," *New York Times*, October 2, 2013, http://www.nytimes.com/2013/10/03/fashion/the-afro-as-a-natural-expression-of-self.html?_r=0; and Danielle C. Belton, "That Afro Is a Lie," The Root, April 2, 2015, http://www.theroot.com/articles/culture/2015/04/politics_of_black_hair_that_afro_is_a_lie.html.

24. Mercer, *Welcome to the Jungle*, 109.

25. Robin D. G. Kelley, *Yo' Mama's Disfunktional! Fighting the Culture Wars in Urban America* (Boston: Beacon, 1997), 37.

26. In 2005 the high school student Kiri Davis replicated the findings of the Clark doll studies in her award-winning short film *A Girl Like Me*, and, similarly, in 2010 CNN commissioned a study by the child psychologist Margaret Beale Spencer that also purported to replicate the Clarks' findings, although the latter study found that white children have significantly more biases toward lighter skin tone than do black children. Jill Billante and Chuck Hadad, "Study: White and Black Children Biased toward Lighter Skin," CNN.com, May 14, 2010, http://www.cnn.com/2010/US/05/13/doll.study/.

27. Gwen Bergner, "Black Children, White Preference: *Brown v. Board*, the Doll Tests, and the Politics of Self-Esteem," *American Quarterly* 61, no. 2 (2009): 299–332, http://www.jstor.org/stable/27734991.

28. Ange-Marie Hancock, *The Politics of Disgust: The Public Identity of the Welfare Queen* (New York: NYU Press, 2004).

29. Dorothy Roberts, *Killing the Black Body: Race, Reproduction, and the Meaning of Liberty* (New York: Vintage Books, 1997).

30. Frank B. Wilderson, *Red, White, and Black: Cinema and the Structure of U.S. Antagonisms* (Durham, NC: Duke University Press, 2010), 65, 58.

31. See, for instance, Jared Sexton, *Amalgamation Schemes: Antiblackness and the Critique of Multiculturalism* (Minneapolis: University of Minnesota Press, 2008); George Yancey, *Who Is White? Latinos, Asians, and the New Black/ Nonblack Divide* (Boulder, CO: Lynne Rienner, 2003); Saidiya V. Hartman, "The Position of the Unthought: An Interview with Saidiya V. Hartman Conducted by Frank B. Wilderson, III," *Qui Parle* 13, no. 2 (2003): 183–201.

32. Wilderson, *Red, White, and Black*, 59.

33. Jared Sexton, "The Social Life of Social Death: On Afro-Pessimism and Black Optimism," *Tensions* 5 (2011): 28–29 (emphasis in original).

34. Spillers interview; Hortense J. Spillers, "The Crisis of the Negro Intellectual: A Post-date," in *Black, White, and in Color: Essays on American Literature and Culture* (Chicago: University of Chicago Press, 2003), 428–70; Hortense Spillers, "'All the Things You Could Be by Now, If Sigmund Freud's Wife Was Your Mother': Psychoanalysis and Race," in *Black, White, and in Color*, 376–427.

35. Elizabeth Alexander, *The Black Interior* (Saint Paul, MN: Graywolf, 2004), x.

36. Toni Morrison, "The Site of Memory," in *Inventing the Truth: The Art and Craft of Memoir*, ed. William Zinsser (Boston: Houghton Mifflin, 1995), 83–102.

37. In this way, I am privileging the analysis of a "politics of culture" over a "culture of politics." Wilderson, *Red, White, and Black*, 26.

38. Ralph Ellison, "The World and the Jug," in *Shadow and Act*, 162.

39. Stuart Hall, "New Ethnicities," in *Stuart Hall: Critical Dialogues in Cultural Studies*, ed. David Morley and Kuan-Hsing Chen (London: Routledge, 1996), 443–44; Herman Gray, *Watching Race: Television and the Struggle for "Blackness"* (Minneapolis: University of Minnesota Press, 1995), 3.

40. The term "archetype-hunting" comes from Ralph Ellison, "Change the Joke and Slip the Yoke," in *Shadow and Act*, 101.

41. Frank Wilderson III, "Gramsci's Black Marx: Whither the Slave in Civil Society?," *Social Identities* 9, no. 2 (2003): 226, 230.

42. Ibid., 238–39 (emphasis in original).

43. Ibid., 231.

44. Ntozake Shange, *Moon Marked and Touched by Sun: Plays by African-American Women*, ed. Sydné Mahone (New York: Theater Communications Group, 1994), 323.

45. Fred Moten, "The Case of Blackness," *Criticism* 50, no. 2 (2008): 188 (emphasis in original). Sexton's article "The Social Life of Social Death" is at least

partially a response to this essay. In it, Moten argues against the notion of social death by way of a discussion of Frantz Fanon that pivots on a distinction between a death-driven nonbeing and a social subject more akin to a Heideggerian being-toward-death. He lingers on the mistranslated title of the fifth chapter of *Black Skins, White Masks*—what would more literally read as "the lived experience of the black" gets translated as "the fact of blackness"—to explore the terrain of meaning that inheres in the break between "blackness" and "the black" and that gets underscored by Fanon's claim that the black (man) is an ontological impossibility, that is, one who can only ever exist in relation to the white (man). Accordingly, what is conceded by Fanon's formulation is that there can be no black social life when blackness is only ever a response to whiteness and is consequently always already pathologized, vacant, or dead, as a result of that correspondence. What eventually comes into view for Moten, then, is a black social life that emerges from the lived experience of the black but that is simultaneously denied by its own supposed impossibility. Ultimately, he argues that "the notion that there is no black social life is part of a set of variations on a theme that include assertions of the irreducible pathology of black social life and the implication that (non-pathological) social life is what emerges by way of the exclusion of the black, or, more precisely, of blackness" (188). The problem of blackness—the formulation of a sociality, a lived experience, that is sustained by its own impossibility—is thus glimpsed via a deeply felt desire to claim that which can only be understood, and negatively embraced, through a process of disavowal. Yet for Moten this is not to dismiss Fanon's ambivalence out of hand but is a means of contemplating what is held by that ambivalence, for Fanon's "almost general refusal to look at the way the colonized look at themselves" (213) is completely bound up with his impulse to reject any notion of an essential, *unpoliticized*, criminality constitutive of the black.

46. Similarly, Cathy Cohen argues the necessity of a "politics of deviance" wherein "we are witness to the power of those at the bottom, whose everyday life decisions challenge, or at least counter, the basic normative assumptions of a society intent on protecting structural and social inequalities under the guise of some normal and natural order to life." Cathy J. Cohen, "Deviance as Resistance: A New Research Agenda for the Study of Black Politics," *Du Bois Review* 1 (2004): 33.

47. She goes on to say, "not thinking is even more dangerous." Hannah Arendt, *The Last Interview and Other Conversations* (Brooklyn, NY: Melville House, 2013), 123.

48. Ta-Nehisi Coates, *Between the World and Me* (New York: Spiegel and Grau, 2015), 34.

49. Spillers talks about this analytic as the distinction between the "individual" and the "one": "I think of it as a way that leads to greater self-consciousness, a

self-critical capacity in your relationship to others because as far as I'm concerned you're always in relationship to others, even when you are a lone figure. . . . I think of the individual as a certain kind of formation in relationship to property. It's a bourgeois or middle-class idea that's associated with liberal property or early modern capital or early modern property. . . . The 'one' is put in place by the social, it is put in place by language, one's relationship to the social, to language, to others." Spillers interview.

50. For a more thorough and multivariate discussion of post-blackness and its critiques, see Houston A. Baker Jr. and K. Merinda Simmons, eds., *The Trouble with Post-Blackness* (New York: Columbia University Press, 2015).

51. Spillers, "Crisis of the Negro Intellectual," 460–61 (emphasis in original).

52. Ibid., 458.

53. Ibid.

54. Ibid., 443.

55. Ibid., 461.

56. All but the final word in this series (which are all defined on urbandictionary .com, one of the great treatises of black social life) are defined in Geneva Smitherman, *Black Talk: Words and Phrases from the Hood to the Amen Corner*, rev. ed. (Boston: Houghton Mifflin, 2000).

57. Jane Bakerman, "The Seams Can't Show: An Interview with Toni Morrison," *Black American Literature Forum* 12, no. 2 (1978): 58.

58. Robin M. Boylorn and Mark P. Orbe, introduction to *Critical Autoethnography: Intersecting Cultural Identities in Everyday Life*, ed. Robin M. Boylorn and Mark P. Orbe (Walnut Creek, CA: Left Coast, 2014), 16–17.

59. Heewon Chang, *Autoethnography as Method* (Walnut Creek, CA: Left Coast, 2008), 49.

60. Spillers, "Crisis of the Negro Intellectual," 458.

61. Victor Anderson, *Creative Exchange: A Constructive Theology of African American Religious Experience* (Minneapolis: Fortress, 2008), chap. 5; Kimberlé Crenshaw, "Mapping the Margins: Intersectionality, Identity Politics, and Violence against Women of Color," *Stanford Law Review* 43 (1991): 1241–99.

62. Toni Morrison, "Home," in *The House that Race Built*, ed. Wahneema Lubiano (New York: Pantheon Books, 1997), 5. See also bell hooks's discussion of home as a site of resistance in "Homeplace: A Site of Resistance," in *Yearning: Race, Gender, and Cultural Politics* (Boston: South End, 1990), 41–49.

63. Daphne A. Brooks, "'All That You Can't Leave Behind': Black Female Soul Singing and the Politics of Surrogation in the Age of Catastrophe," *Meridians* 8, no. 1 (2008): 183, http://www.jstor.org/stable/40338916.

64. Lindon Barrett, *Blackness and Value: Seeing Double* (Cambridge: Cambridge University Press, 1999), 148.

1. ON ANGER

1. Audre Lorde, *Sister Outsider* (Berkeley: Crossing, 1984), 60; Patricia Hill Collins, "Learning from the Outsider Within: The Sociological Significance of Black Female Thought," *Social Problems* 33, no. 6 (1986): S14–S32.

2. Keith Hollihan, "The Omarosa Experiment," *Morning News*, January 17, 2006, http://www.themorningnews.org/article/the-omarosa-experiment.

3. For further discussions of black women and reality television see, for instance, Therí A. Pickens, "Shoving Aside the Politics of Respectability: Black Women, Reality TV, and the Ratchet Performance," *Women & Performance* 25, no. 1 (2015): 41–58; Jervette R. Ward, ed., *Real Sister: Stereotypes, Respectability, and Black Women in Reality TV* (New Brunswick, NJ: Rutgers University Press, 2015); Kristen J. Warner, "They Gon' Think You Loud Regardless: Ratchetness, Reality Television, and Black Womanhood," *Camera Obscura* 30, no. 1 (2015): 129–52; Jennifer L. Pozner, *Reality Bites Back: The Troubling Truth about Guilty Pleasure TV* (Berkeley, CA: Seal, 2010); Robin M. Boylorn, "As Seen on TV: An Autoethnographic Reflection on Race and Reality Television," *Critical Studies in Media Communication* 25, no. 4 (2008): 413–33; Rachel E. Dubrofsky and Antoine Hardy, "Performing Race in *Flavor of Love* and *The Bachelor*," *Critical Studies in Media Communication* 25, no. 4 (2008): 373–92; Kimberly Springer, "Divas, Evil Black Bitches, and Bitter Black Women: African American Women in Post-feminist and Post-Civil-Rights Popular Culture," in *Interrogating Postfeminism: Gender and the Politics of Popular Culture*, ed. Yvonne Tasker and Diane Negra (Durham, NC: Duke University Press, 2007), 249–76.

4. Lorde, *Sister Outsider*, 166–67.

5. Hortense Spillers, interview by Tim Haslett, February 4, 1998, http://www .blackculturalstudies.org/spillers/spillers_intvw.html (site discontinued).

6. Frank Wilderson, *Red, White and Black: Cinema and the Structure of U.S. Antagonisms* (Durham, NC: Duke University Press, 2010), 5.

7. Ibid., 10–11.

8. Ibid., 2.

9. Claudia Rankine, *Citizen: An American Lyric* (Minneapolis: Graywolf, 2014), 23–24.

10. Ibid., 29.

11. Ibid., 24 (emphasis added).

12. Ibid., 35.

13. *Venus and Serena*, directed by Maiken Baird and Michelle Major (Magnolia Pictures, 2012).

14. Here, the word "containing" is meant to reference *both* capacity and restraint.

15. *Oxford English Dictionary Online*, s.v. "anger," accessed May 27, 2015, http://www.oed.com; *Middle English Dictionary Online*, s.v. "anger," accessed

May 27, 2015, http://quod.lib.umich.edu/m/med/; *Online Etymology Dictionary*, s.v. "anger," accessed May 27, 2015, http://www.etymonline.com.

16. Stefano Harney and Fred Moten, *The Undercommons: Fugitive Planning and Black Study* (Brooklyn, NY: Autonomedia, 2013), 109.

17. Ibid.

18. Ibid., 112.

19. Moten supposes what would happen if, as a teacher, he walked into the classroom and, rather than acting as an "instrument of government," noted the fact that study was happening even before he entered the room and, "instead of announcing that class has begun, just acknowledged that class began." Ibid., 125–26.

20. Jane Bakerman, "The Seams Can't Show: An Interview with Toni Morrison," *Black American Literature Forum* 12, no. 2 (1978): 57.

21. Toni Morrison, foreword to *Sula* (New York: Vintage, 2004), xiv–xv. Further references to the novel are cited parenthetically in the text.

22. For a discussion of various ways black women use "girl" and some of the more contemporary controversies around its usage, see Veronica Wells, "Our Favorite Word? . . . Girl," *Madame Noire*, January 10, 2012, http://madamenoire .com/127461/our-favorite-word-girl/.

23. Candice Jenkins, *Private Lives, Proper Relations: Regulating Black Intimacy* (Minneapolis: University of Minnesota Press, 2007), 77–78 (emphasis in original).

24. Ibid., 78. As discussed in chapter 5 of this text, Lindon Barrett makes a similar argument about Lutie Johnson, the protagonist of Ann Petry's *The Street*.

25. Hortense J. Spillers, "A Hateful Passion, a Love Lost: Three Women's Fiction," in *Black, White, and in Color: Essays on American Literature and Culture* (Chicago: University of Chicago Press, 2003), 93, 118 (emphasis in original).

26. Jenkins refers to this as a "long masked . . . correspondence between the two women" (*Private Lives*, 85).

27. Toni Morrison, interview by Thomas LeClair, "The Language Must Not Sweat," *New Republic*, March 21, 1981.

28. Spillers, "Hateful Passion," 94.

29. Ibid., 95.

30. Ibid.

31. Lorde, *Sister Outsider*, 132.

2. GETTING HAPPY

1. My use of the term "black church" herein is not meant to reference a specific institution but a particular *tradition* that "possesses distinctive characteristics and constitutive elements, including key questions, symbols, rituals, ideas, and beliefs that are always subject to adaptation, improvisation, reinterpretation, and

even abandonment." Stacey M. Floyd-Thomas, Juan Floyd-Thomas, Carol B. Duncan, Stephen G. Ray Jr., and Nancy Lynne Westfield, *Black Church Studies: An Introduction* (Nashville, TN: Abingdon, 2007), xxiv.

2. James Baldwin, *The Fire Next Time* (1963; repr., New York: Vintage, 1993), 17–18.

3. James Baldwin, *Go Tell It on the Mountain* (1952; repr., New York: Dial, 2005), 60.

4. Ibid., 222.

5. Tonéx, interview by Lexi Allen, *The Lexi Show*, The Word Network, September 5, 2009.

6. Kalefa Sanneh, "Revelations: A Gospel Singer Comes Out," *New Yorker*, February 8, 2010.

7. Tonéx, interview by Darian Aaron, YouTube video, 6:52, posted by "darianout-loud," September 23, 2009, https://www.youtube.com/watch?v=6rz47oZhP_8.

8. I am mindful of Roderick A. Ferguson's argument in regards to black sexuality as conceived within the American social order that holds that "as figures of nonheteronormative perversions, straight African Americans [are] reproductive rather than *productive*, heterosexual but never *heteronormative*." Roderick A. Ferguson, *Aberrations in Black: Toward a Queer of Color Critique* (Minneapolis: University of Minnesota Press, 2004), 87 (emphasis in original). Thus my use of the word "normative" here is strictly relative to the black church context in which it is operationalized.

9. Lindon Barrett, *Blackness and Value: Seeing Double* (Cambridge: Cambridge University Press, 1999), 21.

10. Ibid.

11. C. Riley Snorton, *Nobody Is Supposed to Know: Black Sexuality on the Down Low* (Minneapolis: University of Minnesota Press, 2014), 98.

12. Ibid., 94.

13. Ibid., 95.

14. Shayne Lee defines neo-Pentecostalism in his book on T. D. Jakes as "the contemporary form of the Pentecostal movement that emerged in the latter part of the twentieth century"; it puts less emphasis on puritanical asceticism, speaking in tongues, etc., and more emphasis on "the power of the Holy Spirit for healing, prophetic utterances, vibrant worship and music, and prosperity for believers." Shayne Lee, *T. D. Jakes: America's New Preacher* (New York: NYU Press, 2005), 34. For a concise discussion of the history of black Pentecostalism in the United States and its relationship to prosperity gospel, see Fredrick C. Harris, "Entering the Land of Milk and Honey," in *The Price of the Ticket: Barack Obama and the Rise and Decline of Black Politics* (New York: Oxford University Press, 2012), 70–99.

15. Libby Copeland, "With Gifts from God," *Washington Post*, March 25, 2001.

16. Apparently all was not always well between Jakes and Bynum, however. A legal dispute over royalties arose between the two after Jakes began selling tapes of Bynum's sermon, and this reportedly resulted in Jakes temporarily blacklisting Bynum from preaching at prominent black churches and venues. The matter was eventually resolved after Jakes invited Bynum to another of his conferences and Bynum issued Jakes a public apology. Lee, *T. D. Jakes*, 149–50.

17. Denene Millner, "I've Come This Far by Faith," *Essence*, December 2007; Denene Millner, "Dawn of a New Day," *Essence*, January 2008.

18. Rosalind Bentley, "For 'Prophetess' of Romance, Marriage a Mess," *Atlanta Journal-Constitution*, August 26, 2007.

19. Juanita Bynum, *No More Sheets* (Waycross, GA: Juanita Bynum Ministries, n.d.), DVD. All sermon quotes are from this source.

20. Candice Jenkins, *Private Lives, Proper Relations: Regulating Black Intimacy* (Minneapolis: University of Minnesota Press, 2007), 12–16.

21. E. Patrick Johnson, "Feeling the Spirit in the Dark: Expanding Notions of the Sacred in the African-American Gay Community," *Callaloo* 21, no. 2 (1998): 399–416.

22. Ibid., 413.

23. Ashon Crawley, "Circum-Religious Performance: Queer(ed) Black Bodies and the Black Church," *Theology and Sexuality* 14, no. 2 (2008): 217.

24. See Fred Moten, *The Feel Trio* (Tucson, AZ: Letter Machine Editions), 65–93.

25. Crawley, "Circum-Religious Performance," 216.

26. Ibid., 217.

27. Ibid., 216–17.

28. Audre Lorde, "Uses of the Erotic: The Erotic as Power," in *Sister Outsider: Essays and Speeches by Audre Lorde*, rev. ed. (Berkeley, CA: Crossing, 2007), 53.

29. Ibid., 57.

30. Barrett, *Blackness and Value*, 65, 87.

31. Baldwin, *Fire Next Time*, 41.

3. THE WAY IT IS

1. See, for instance, Daphne Brooks's discussion of Terry McMillan as contributing to "the construction and visibility of a Black middle-class female consumer." Daphne A. Brooks, "It's Not Right but It's Okay: Black Women's R&B and the House that Terry McMillan Built," *Souls* 5, no. 1 (2003): 33–34.

2. Although, it should be mentioned, the professed sexual relationships of the named artists have been almost exclusively heterosexual.

3. James Baldwin, *The Fire Next Time* (New York: Vintage International, 1993), 43.

4. Ibid., 41.

5. Chaka Khan, "I'm Every Woman," written by Nickolas Ashford and Valerie Simpson, on *Chaka* (Warner Brothers, 1978).

6. Marcia Ann Gillespie, "The Myth of the Strong Black Woman," in *Feminist Frameworks: Alternative Theoretical Accounts of the Relations between Women and Men*, 2nd ed., ed. Alison M. Jaggar and Paula S. Rothenberg (New York: McGraw-Hill, 1984), 33.

7. Meg Henson Scales, "Tenderheaded, or Rejecting the Legacy of Being able to Take It," in *Tenderheaded: A Comb-Bending Collection of Hair Stories*, ed. Juliette Harris and Pamela Johnson (New York: Pocket Books, 2001), 31.

8. Gillespie, "Myth of the Strong Black Woman," 34; Trudier Harris, *Saints, Sinners, Saviors: Strong Black Women in African American Literature* (New York: Palgrave, 2001); Patricia Hill Collins, *Black Sexual Politics: African Americans, Gender, and the New Racism* (New York: Routledge, 2005), 208–9; Joan Morgan, *When Chickenheads Come Home to Roost: A Hip-Hop Feminist Breaks It Down* (New York: Simon and Schuster, 1999), 87. Both Hill Collins and Morgan specifically address heterosexual relationships.

9. But see Sheri Parks's discussion of the "Sacred Dark Feminine" and her argument that the beginnings of human existence are the strong black woman's point of origin. Sheri Parks, *Fierce Angels: The Strong Black Woman in American Life and Culture* (New York: One World Books, 2010).

10. Harris, *Saints, Sinners, Saviors*, 19.

11. Henson Scales, "Tenderheaded," 31; Melissa Harris-Perry, *Sister Citizen: Shame, Stereotypes, and Black Women in America* (New Haven, CT: Yale University Press, 2011), 216; Tamara Beauboeuf-Lafontant, "Strong and Large Black Women: Exploring Relationships between Deviant Womanhood and Weight," *Gender & Society* 17, no. 1 (2003): 111.

12. Harris-Perry also argues, however, that "there does seem to be room in black public opinion for acceptance of black women who need help to meet life's many demands." Melissa Harris-Lacewell, "No Place to Rest: African American Political Attitudes and the Myth of Black Women's Strength," *Women and Politics* 23 (2001): 24–25.

13. Tamara Beauboeuf-Lafontant, *Behind the Mask of the Strong Black Woman: Voice and the Embodiment of a Costly Performance* (Philadelphia: Temple University Press, 2009).

14. Hortense Spillers, "Interstices: A Small Drama of Words," in *Black, White, and in Color: Essays on American Literature and Culture* (Chicago: University of Chicago Press, 2003), 167.

15. Ibid., 165.

16. Ibid., 167.

17. Brooks, "It's Not Right but It's Okay," 41.

18. Elizabeth Alexander, *The Black Interior* (Saint Paul, MN: Graywolf, 2004), x.

19. Ibid., 6.

20. Ibid., 7.

21. Daphne A. Brooks, "'All That You Can't Leave Behind': Black Female Soul Singing and the Politics of Surrogation in the Age of Catastrophe," *Meridians* 8, no. 1 (2008): 183, http://www.jstor.org/stable/40338916.

22. Delores S. Williams, "Social-Role Surrogacy: Naming Black Women's Oppression," chap. 3 in *Sisters in the Wilderness: The Challenge of Womanist God-Talk* (Maryknoll, NY: Orbis Books, 1993); Brooks, "All That You Can't Leave Behind," 183.

23. Spillers, "Interstices," 168, 173.

24. Houston Baker, "Critical Memory and the Black Public Sphere," in *The Black Public Sphere: A Public Culture Book*, ed. Black Public Sphere Collective (Chicago: University of Chicago Press, 1995), 13, 15.

25. Stuart Hall, "What Is This 'Black' In Black Popular Culture?," in *Stuart Hall: Critical Dialogues in Cultural Studies*, ed. David Morley and Kuan-Hsing Chen (London: Routledge, 1996), 470.

26. Herman Gray, "Cultural Politics as Outrage(ous)," *Black Renaissance / Renaissance Noire* 3 (2000): 97.

27. Chad Raphael, "The Political Economic Origins of Reali-TV," in *Reality TV: Remaking Television Culture*, 2nd ed., ed. Susan Murray and Laurie Ouellette (New York: NYU Press, 2009), 123–40.

28. "If I Can You Can," *Keyshia Cole: The Way It Is*, season 1, episode 1 (Geffen Records, 2008), DVD.

29. *Keyshia Cole: The Way It Is: The Complete Second Season*, Black Entertainment Television (Paramount Pictures, 2008), DVD. Interestingly, Cole is described here as both a "hip-hop superstar" and an "R&B star," which is illustrative of how she is being actively positioned as the successor to the "Queen of Hip Hop Soul," Mary J. Blige.

30. For years BET was beleaguered by complaints that its programming demeaned and misrepresented black people and black business interests. In the 1990s and early 2000s critics took aim at the network's heavy use of rap music videos to fill airtime. After the network aired rap artist Nelly's now-infamous "Tip Drill" video on its late-night video show *Uncut* in 2004, students, faculty, and administrators at Spelman College protested and eventually had canceled an appearance the rapper had scheduled on campus to conduct a bone-marrow drive in honor of his sister. The network also drew fire in 2006 when it failed to preempt its programming to air the funeral of Coretta Scott King and again in 2007 when it aired a show originally titled *Hot Ghetto Mess* that was changed before its premiere

to *We Got to Do Better* amid protests that the show was meant primarily to deal in black stereotypes—an argument that is echoed in complaints about BET's purported overuse of black sitcoms like *Sanford and Son* and *The Jamie Foxx Show* in its programming lineup. See, for instance, Lee Hubbard, "Blacks, BET and Boycotts," AlterNet.org, December 19, 2001, http://www.alternet.org/story /12129/blacks%2C_bet_and_boycotts; Chloé A. Hilliard, "Hot Ghetto BET," *Village Voice*, August 22, 2007; Eric Deggans and Lynette R. Holloway, "The New BET," *Ebony*, October 2007, 216–27; Felicia R. Lee, "Protesting Demeaning Images in Media," *New York Times*, November 5, 2007; Rozena Henderson, "BET, Are You Listening?," *New Pittsburgh Courier*, July 16, 2008; Kristal Brent Zook, "Has Reality TV Become Black Women's Enemy?," The Root, May 24, 2010, http://www .theroot.com/views/has-reality-tv-become-black-women-s-enemy; Boyce Watkins, "Why There Should Be a Backlash against BET," theGrio, June 28, 2010, http:// thegrio.com/2010/06/28/why-there-should-be-a-black-backlash-against-bet/.

31. Mesfin Fekadu, "Keyshia Cole Still Growing," *New Pittsburgh Courier*, January 5, 2011; Kelley L. Carter, "No More Drama," *Essence*, October 2012, 71.

32. Joseph Roach, *Cities of the Dead: Circum-Atlantic Performance* (New York: Columbia University Press, 1996), 6.

33. "No More Tears, Mama!," *Keyshia Cole: The Way It Is: The Complete Second Season*, episode 2, aired November 6, 2007.

34. Ibid.

35. "Full Circle," *Keyshia Cole: The Way It Is*, season 3, episode 8, aired December 23, 2008, iTunes video.

36. "No More Tears, Mama!"

37. Laurie Ouellette, "'Take Responsibility for Yourself': Judge Judy and the Neoliberal Citizen," in Murray and Ouellette, *Reality TV*, 224.

38. Anna McCarthy, "Reality Television: A Neoliberal Theater of Suffering," *Social Text* 25, no. 4 (2007): 25, doi: 10.1215/01642472-2007-010.

39. Ibid., 32

40. Ibid., 33.

41. Ibid., 25.

42. "Music Is My Hustle!," *Keyshia Cole: The Way It Is: The Complete Second Season*, episode 1, aired October 30, 2007.

43. Lindon Barrett, *Blackness and Value: Seeing Double* (Cambridge: Cambridge University Press, 1999), 56, 58.

44. Ibid., 83.

45. Kara Keeling, *The Witch's Flight: The Cinematic, the Black Femme, and the Image of Common Sense* (Durham, NC: Duke University Press, 2007), 136.

46. Spillers, "Interstices," 166.

4. BABY MAMA

1. U.S. Department of Health and Human Services, *Vital Statistics of the United States, 1987* (Hyattsville, MD: U.S. Department of Health and Human Services, 1989); U.S. Department of Health and Human Services, *Vital Statistics of the United States, 1988* (Hyattsville, MD: U.S. Department of Health and Human Services, 1990).

2. Molly Parker, "Too Taboo? Peoria Area Struggles to Rein in Epidemic," *Journal Star* (Peoria, IL), May 20, 2007.

3. These statistics, complied from U.S. Vital Statistics records, are based on cities with populations of one hundred thousand or more.

4. T. J. Mathews, Paul D. Sutton, Brady E. Hamilton, and Stephanie J. Ventura, *State Disparities in Teenage Birth Rates in the United States*, data brief 46 (Hyattsville, MD: National Center for Health Statistics, October 2010). When not taking into account city population, the southeastern states of Arkansas, Louisiana, Tennessee, and Mississippi are also among the top-ten states with the highest birth rates among black teenagers. The other six states are Ohio, Illinois, Wisconsin, Nebraska, Iowa, and Minnesota. Ibid.

5. Dean Olsen, "Grants Aim to Combat Teen Pregnancy," *Journal Star* (Peoria, IL), March 23, 1996.

6. Dean Olsen, "Positive Peer Pressure Helps Girls Avoid Pregnancy Trap," *Journal Star* (Peoria, IL), February 9, 1994.

7. Dean Olsen, "Teen Motherhood Runs in Family," *Journal Star* (Peoria, IL), February 6, 1994.

8. Dean Olsen, "Many Black Leaders Critical of Unwed Parenthood Series," *Journal Star* (Peoria, IL), February 20, 1994.

9. Linda Henson, "Get Mad: Do Something for Peoria's Unwed Teens," *Journal Star* (Peoria, IL), February 15, 1994.

10. Shari Mannery, "It's a Disgrace: Too Many People Are Ranting and Raving over a Photo," *Journal Star* (Peoria, IL), February 15, 1994.

11. Dean Olsen, "Curing Teen Pregnancy: A Long-Term Delivery," *Journal Star* (Peoria, IL), August 18, 1997.

12. Similarly, in a discussion of the assertions made by individuals purportedly concerned about the problems attendant to children born to drug-addicted black mothers, Dorothy Roberts argues, "the primary concern of this sort of rhetoric is typically the huge cost these children impose on taxpayers, rather than the children's welfare." Dorothy Roberts, *Killing the Black Body* (New York: Vintage, 1997), 20.

13. Lindon Barrett, *Blackness and Value: Seeing Double* (Cambridge: Cambridge University Press, 1999), 143, quoting Mark Taylor, *Erring: A Postmodern A/theology* (Chicago: University of Chicago Press, 1984), 159.

14. This is, admittedly, a controversial claim, as the nature of the grotesque has been taken up across a wide range of intellectual fields of inquiry and has been used to address a diverse range of subjects. But because a full accounting of the various theorizations of the grotesque that abound in academic literature, even just in relationship to U.S. subject positions or American fiction, is beyond the scope of my project here, I constrain my current discussion to Barrett's useful conceptualization of the term as it pertains to the particularities of blackness in the U.S. sociocultural imaginary.

15. Toni Morrison, "Unspeakable Things Unspoken: The Afro-American Presence in American Literature," *Michigan Quarterly Review* 28, no. 1 (1989): 12.

16. Barrett, *Blackness and Value*, 150.

17. Ibid., 144.

18. I am using "hypervisuality" here in the sense of Nicole Fleetwood, who defines the term as a reference to "both historic and contemporary conceptualizations of blackness as simultaneously invisible and always visible, as underexposed and always exposed, the nuances of which have been depicted in art, literature, and theory." Nicole Fleetwood, *Troubling Vision: Performance, Visuality, and Blackness* (Chicago: University of Chicago Press, 2011), 111. An elaboration of this point can be found in the work of Avery Gordon, who suggests that "hypervisibility is a kind of obscenity of accuracy that abolishes the distinctions between 'permission and prohibition, presence and absence.'" Avery Gordon, *Ghostly Matters: Haunting and the Sociological Imagination*, rev. ed. (Minneapolis: University of Minnesota Press, 2008), 16, quoting Laura Kipnis, "Feminism: The Political Conscious of Postmodernism?," in *Universal Abandon? The Politics of Postmodernism*, ed. Andrew Ross (Minneapolis: University of Minnesota Press, 1988), 158.

19. Frantz Fanon, *Black Skin, White Masks* (New York: Grove, 1952), xv. Stuart Hall defines *epidermalization* as "literally, the inscription of race on the skin." Stuart Hall, "The After-life of Frantz Fanon: Why Fanon? Why Now? Why *Black Skin, White Masks*?," in *The Fact of Blackness: Frantz Fanon and Visual Representation*, ed. Alan Read (Seattle: Bay, 1996), 16.

20. Hortense J. Spillers, "Mama's Baby, Papa's Maybe: An American Grammar Book," in *Black, White, and in Color: Essays on American Literature and Culture* (Chicago: University of Chicago Press, 2003), 205.

21. Barrett, *Blackness and Value*, 130.

22. Ibid., 148–49, quoting Gauri Viswanathan, *Masks of Conquest: Literary Study and British Rule in India* (New York: Columbia University Press, 1989), 85.

23. Ibid., 142.

24. See, for example, Frank F. Furstenberg, *Destinies of the Disadvantaged: The Politics of Teenage Childbearing* (New York: Russell Sage Foundation, 2007); Arline T. Geronimus, "Damned If You Do: Culture, Identity, Privilege, and

Teenage Childbearing in the United States," *Social Science and Medicine* 57 (2003): 881–93; V. Joseph Hotz, Susan Williams McElroy, and Seth G. Sanders, "The Costs and Consequences of Teenage Childbearing for the Mothers and the Government," *Chicago Policy Review* 64 (Fall 1996): 55–94; Kristin Luker, *Dubious Conceptions: The Politics of Teenage Pregnancy* (Cambridge, MA: Harvard University Press, 1996); Constance A. Nathanson, *Dangerous Passage: The Social Control of Sexuality in Women's Adolescence* (Philadelphia: Temple University Press, 1993); Kristin Luker, "Dubious Conceptions: The Controversy over Teen Pregnancy," *American Prospect* 5 (Spring 1991): 73–83.

25. Luker, *Dubious Conceptions*, 71–80. The Pregnancy Prevention Act was ultimately superseded in 1981 by the Adolescent Family Life Act (aka the "chastity bill"), which, unlike the previous bills, targeted both teenagers and their parents while also restricting access to abortion and promoting adoption as an alternative and proposing sex education as a deterrent to premarital sex. Ibid.; Furstenberg, *Destinies of the Disadvantaged*, 87.

26. Furstenberg, *Destinies of the Disadvantaged*, 12 (emphasis in original).

27. Ibid., 17.

28. Luker, *Dubious Conceptions*, 82.

29. As noted earlier, the 1950s saw the highest teenage pregnancy and childbearing rates, which then began to decline after the baby-boom years. Although the overall pregnancy rate was declining, teenage pregnancy rates began trending moderately upward again in the 1980s due at least in part to less restrictive attitudes toward sex. After peaking in 1991, rates again began to fall substantially, and in 2004 they fell to their lowest level in half a century. There was a slight increase from 2005 to 2007 before rates began to decline again in 2008 and 2009. Furstenberg, *Destinies of the Disadvantaged*, 83, 94; Gladys Martinez, Casey E. Copen, and Joyce C. Abma, "Teenagers in the United States: Sexual Activity, Contraceptive Use, and Childbearing, 2006–2010 National Survey of Family Growth," *Vital and Health Statistics* 23, no. 31 (Hyattsville, MD: National Center for Health Statistics, October 2011).

30. Luker, *Dubious Conceptions*, 82–83 (emphasis added).

31. What is true as well is that "since 1985 birthrates among unmarried white teenagers have been increasing rapidly, while those among unmarried black teens have been largely stable." Ibid., 7.

32. Traditional beliefs about the educational outcomes of teenage mothers and the health outcomes of their children are challenged here as well.

33. Luker, *Dubious Conceptions*, 80.

34. Hotz, Williams McElroy, and Sanders, "Costs and Consequences."

35. Candice Jenkins, *Private Lives, Proper Relations: Regulating Black Intimacy* (Minneapolis: University of Minnesota Press, 2007), 11, quoting Wahneema Lubiano, "Black Ladies, Welfare Queens, and State Minstrels: Ideological War by

Narrative Means," in *Race-ing Justice, En-Gendering Power*, ed. Toni Morrison (New York: Pantheon, 1992), 339.

36. Furstenberg, *Destinies of the Disadvantaged*, 50.

37. Ibid., 46–52.

38. Geronimus, "Damned If You Do," 885 (emphasis in original).

39. Dean Olsen, "Mom Tried to Help End a Pattern," *Journal Star* (Peoria, IL), February 10, 1994.

40. Editorial, "Responsibility, Jobs, Hope," *Journal Star* (Peoria, IL), February 14, 1994.

41. Ibid.

42. Dean Olsen, "Why Peoria? Birthrates Rose with Financial Strife in '80s," *Journal Star* (Peoria, IL), February 7, 1994.

43. My own parents were impacted by this economic downturn. My mother was working as the presidential secretary of UAW Local 974, the union that represents Caterpillar's employees, when she was laid off in 1985. She was rehired in January 1988 after another employee retired, and in December of that year she became the union's bookkeeper, a position she still holds to this day. Also during this time period my father, from whom my mother was by then divorced, was laid off from Sealtest Dairy, the first job he acquired after migrating north from West Memphis, Arkansas.

44. Olsen, "Why Peoria?" Similarly, by 1983 another Illinois city, Rockford, had one of the highest, if not *the* highest, unemployment rates among metro areas in the country at 25 percent. It simultaneously had one of the highest rates of unwed black mothers in the country. Samantha Ptashkin, "Rockford Unemployment: Better Off Now or in the 1980s?," WREX.com, March 17, 2010, http://www.wrex.com/Global/story.asp?S=12158573.

45. Editorial, "Responsibility, Jobs, Hope."

46. Chia Freeman, "Deadbeats? Some of Us Have Little Choice," *Journal Star* (Peoria, IL), February 20, 1994.

47. Olsen, "Mom Tried to Help End a Pattern."

48. Furstenberg, *Destinies of the Disadvantaged*, 110.

49. Leopoldina Fortunati, *The Arcane of Reproduction: Housework, Prostitution, Labor and Capital*, ed. Jim Fleming, trans. Hilary Creek (Brooklyn, NY: Autonomedia, 1995), 10.

50. Ibid., 8 (emphasis in original).

51. Ibid., 10 (emphasis in original).

52. Ibid., 9.

53. Ibid., 24.

54. "The Position of the Unthought: An Interview with Saidiya V. Hartman Conducted by Frank B. Wilderson, III," *Qui Parle* 13, no. 2 (2003): 183–201.

55. Frank B. Wilderson III, *Red, White, and Black: Cinema and the Structure of U.S. Antagonisms* (Durham, NC: Duke University Press, 2010), 14, 37.

56. Ibid., 45.

57. "Position of the Unthought," 187.

58. Barrett, *Blackness and Value*, 146.

59. Aliyyah I. Abdur-Rahman, *Against the Closet: Black Political Longing and the Erotics of Race* (Durham, NC: Duke University Press, 2012), 6.

60. Barrett, *Blackness and Value*, 139.

5. IN THE LIFE

1. Between 2000 and 2011 the death penalty was on moratorium in Illinois. The Illinois death penalty was eventually abolished on March 9, 2011, but until that date the state continued to seek death sentences. The death penalty was therefore still a viable bargaining chip in 2006 when Bright was sentenced. Bright confessed to murdering eight of the nine women murdered between 2003 and 2004. Wanda Jackson (forty) was found strangled to death on March 21, 2001. Frederickia Brown (twenty-nine) went missing on Christmas Eve of 2003, and her decomposed body was discovered in a field two months later. Although the deaths of Wanda and Frederickia were similar to the those of the other women and they shared a similar background with Bright's victims, because Bright denied having any involvement in their deaths and there was no forensic evidence to link the women to him, their deaths remain unsolved and they are not officially considered Bright's victims, though unofficially many residents do still refer to them as Bright's victims. Leslie Williams, "Suspect's Arrest Is Adding Questions—Case Quandary: If Larry Bright Says He Didn't Kill Peorians Wanda Jackson and Frederickia Brown, Then Who Did?," *Journal Star* (Peoria, IL), February 1, 2005.

2. Michael Awkward, *Burying Don Imus: Anatomy of a Scapegoat* (Minneapolis: University of Minnesota Press, 2009).

3. Hortense Spillers, "'All the Things You Could Be by Now, If Sigmund Freud's Wife Was Your Mother': Psychoanalysis and Race," in *Black, White, and in Color: Essays on American Literature and Culture* (Chicago: University of Chicago Press, 2003), 377; Elizabeth Alexander, *The Black Interior* (Saint Paul, MN: Graywolf, 2004).

4. Associated Press, "Rutgers Women's Team, Coach Speak Out," ESPN.com, April 10, 2007, http://espn.go.com/ncw/news/story?id=2831636.

5. "Statement by NCAA President Myles Brand and Rutgers University President Richard L. McCormick Regarding Comments by MNBC's Don Imus," news release, *Rutgers Today*, April 5, 2007, http://news.rutgers.edu/news-releases /2007/04/statement-by-ncaa-pr-20070405#.Vxon13CIQ-9.

6. The number of victims in each of these cases ranges from three to more than twenty, and in larger cities such as Los Angeles, Chicago, and Detroit there has been overlap among active serial killers across time periods and within particular geographic locations. The Peoria case is an outlier in that the perpetrator was a white man, but in almost every other instance when the killers of black women in serial murder cases are known, they are black men. Usually when I am referring to "black serial murder" here, I am talking about cases in which at least three people, all or most of them black women, were killed in separate incidents by the same person. Because my approach to serial murder is victim centered, however, I do also consider cases in which a series of similar murders have been attributed to more than one perpetrator, even when those perpetrators are not themselves considered serial murderers. An example of this would be the 1979 Boston murders around which the black feminist organization the Combahee River Collective was very active. In that case the bodies of twelve black women and one white woman were found murdered and discarded within a two-mile radius in the city in less than six months. Seven different men were eventually arrested in conjunction with the murders. Two of those men were ultimately convicted in three of the deaths, another man was acquitted in a fourth death, and the murders of the other women went unsolved. Despite this, there remained lingering concern in the community that the wrong man or men may have been convicted and that the deaths might actually have been the work of a single killer. Either way, for my purposes I still consider what happened in Boston a serial murder case given the circumstances of the women's deaths. For a detailed discussion of the Boston case see Jaime Grant, "Who's Killing Us?," in *Femicide: The Politics of Woman Killing*, ed. Jill Radford and Diana E. H. Russell (New York: Twayne, 1992), 145–60.

7. James Baldwin, *Notes of a Native Son* (Boston: Beacon, 1955), 27–28.

8. Ibid., 38.

9. Ibid., 27.

10. Lisa Marie Cacho, *Social Death: Racialized Rightlessness and the Criminalization of the Unprotected* (New York: NYU Press, 2012), 8.

11. Ibid., 4.

12. Carmea Erving, telephone interview with the author, November 30, 2007.

13. Bright's confession read, "I know that I have committed some horrific and unthinkable acts. I am very sorry for the grief and the heartache that I have caused." Andy Kravetz, "Relief and Anger: Peorian Will Spend Rest of Life in Prison," *Journal Star* (Peoria, IL), May 31, 2006.

14. Matt Dayhoff, "Prostitute Flees Deadly Grip: A Peoria Woman Recounts Her Night with Slaying Suspect Larry Bright, Saying He Promised Drugs and Read Her Miranda Rights," *Journal Star* (Peoria, IL), February 4, 2005.

15. Jared L. Olar, "Another Woman Reported Missing," *Pekin (IL) Daily Times*, October 29, 2004.

16. Dave Haney, "Serial Killer Task Force Dwindles: Most Detectives Now on to Other Cases, but Still Seek Any Information, Tips," *Journal Star* (Peoria, IL), April 9, 2005. The $20,000 reward was never paid out despite the fact that Vicki Bomar provided information essential to the case and testified in front of a grand jury preceding Bright's indictment. Mike McCoy, the Peoria County sheriff, claimed that although she was "an integral part of the investigation," Bomar did not qualify for the reward because she did not initially go to police on her own accord. She was contacted by police after residents at the shelter she was staying in told them about her encounter with Bright, which she had told them about a couple of months later, and suggested they speak to her. Bomar allegedly did not contact police because she was concerned about two outstanding warrants she had at the time and because she didn't believe the killer would be someone who lived among them on the South Side. McCoy was "baffled" that Bomar and other women in the life hadn't beat down his door to provide information once the reward was announced, especially after police had put out the word that they were not concerned about the women's warrants. What McCoy (and/or the reporting journalist) failed to account for, however, is the mistrust that many women in the life, particularly women of color, feel toward the police and the secrecy that mistrust engenders. Nor did he account for the very real fear the women may have had about becoming victims themselves if they revealed anything about the potential, but still unknown, killer. He also did not account for the emotional and psychological trauma that prevents many people, whether they are in the life or not, from reporting rape and sexual abuse. Phil Luciano, "No One Gets Bright Reward," *Journal Star* (Peoria, IL), July 4, 2006, http://www.pjstar.com /x1021284086/Luciano-No-one-gets-Bright-reward.

17. Leslie Williams, "Blacks: Force Formed Too Late: More Detectives Added in Search for Killer of African-American Women," *Journal Star* (Peoria, IL), October 26, 2004; Sarah Okeson, "Peorians Weep for Lost Women: At Church Forum, Participants Discuss Unsolved Cases and Pray for Their Loved Ones," *Journal Star* (Peoria, IL), November 9, 2004.

18. Carmea and Tyrhonda went on to say that their mother's business partner closed the restaurant down after her death and moved out of town.

19. Tracy Quan, "The Name of the Prose: A Sex Worker by Any Other Name?," in *Prostitution and Pornography: Philosophical Debate about the Sex Industry*, ed. Jessica Spector (Stanford, CA: Stanford University Press, 2006), 343.

20. Hortense J. Spillers, "Mama's Baby, Papa's Maybe: An American Grammar Book," in *Black, White, and in Color*, 203.

21. Toni Morrison, "Unspeakable Things Unspoken: The Afro-American Presence in American Literature," *Michigan Quarterly Review* 28 (1989): 1–34.

22. Avery F. Gordon, *Ghostly Matters: Haunting and the Sociological Imagination* (Minneapolis: University of Minnesota Press, 1997).

23. Toni Morrison, *Beloved* (New York: Vintage, 1987), 333–34.

24. Morrison, "Unspeakable Things Unspoken," 11–12.

25. John Langston Gwaltney, *Drylongso: A Self-Portrait of Black America* (New York: New Press, 1993), 11–13.

26. Cacho, *Social Death*, 13.

27. Stefano Harney and Fred Moten, *The Undercommons: Fugitive Planning and Black Study* (Brooklyn, NY: Autonomedia, 2013).

28. Morrison, *Beloved*, xvii.

29. Ibid., 8.

30. Jack Halberstam, "The Wild Beyond: With and for the Undercommons," foreword to Harney and Moten, *Undercommons*, 11.

31. Gordon, *Ghostly Matters*, 17.

32. Lindon Barrett, *Blackness and Value: Seeing Double* (Cambridge: Cambridge University Press, 1999), 30.

33. Ibid., 120, quoting Gayle Rubin, "Thinking Sex: Notes for a Radical Theory of the Politics of Sexuality," in *The Lesbian and Gay Studies Reader*, ed. Henry Abelove, Michèle Aina Barale, and David M. Halperin (New York: Routledge, 1993), 19.

34. Ann Petry, *The Street* (1946; repr., New York: Houghton Mifflin, 1998), 66.

35. Ibid., 45.

36. Barrett, *Blackness and Value*, 122.

37. Ibid., 28.

38. Ibid., 128.

39. C. Riley Snorton, *Nobody Is Supposed to Know: Black Sexuality on the Down Low* (Minneapolis: University of Minnesota Press, 2014), 13–14.

40. Cathy J. Cohen, "Punks, Bulldaggers, and Welfare Queens: The Radical Potential of Queer Politics?," *GLQ* 3 (1997): 455.

41. Cacho, *Social Death*, 149.

42. Peter Holley, "After Years of Resistance, Richard Pryor Finally Gets a Hometown Statue," *Washington Post*, May 3, 2015.

43. Jonathan Wright, "Humor and Humanity: The Legacy of Richard Pryor," *Art and Society*, May–June 2013, http://www.peoriamagazines.com/as/2013/may-jun/humor-humanity-legacy-richard-pryor; Nick Vlahos, "Richard Pryor Jr. 'Overwhelmed' by Statue Effort," *Journal Star* (Peoria, IL), May 24, 2014.

44. Amy Groh, "The Phrase That Put Peoria on the Map," *Interbusiness Issues*, June 2009, http://www.peoriamagazines.com/ibi/2009/jun/phrase-put-peoria-map.

45. Richard Pryor, interview by David Felton, October 10, 1974, *No Pryor Restraint: Life in Concert*, disc 3, *1974–1975* (Shout! Factory, 2013).

46. John A. Williams and Dennis A. Williams, *If I Stop I'll Die: The Comedy and Tragedy of Richard Pryor* (New York: Thunder's Mouth, 1991), vi.

47. Richard Pryor with Todd Gold, *Pryor Convictions and Other Life Sentences* (New York: Pantheon Books, 1995), 108.

48. Gordon, *Ghostly Matters*, 183.

AFTERWORD

1. The World Foot Locker store I worked at, like most if not all of the other World Foot Lockers once in existence, has since been modified down to a significantly smaller version of its former self and stripped of its "World" status. Thus the shoe store that became, for better and for worse, my home away from home during my college years no longer actually exists.

2. James Baldwin, "James Baldwin—Reflections of a Maverick," interview by Julius Lester, in *James Baldwin: The Last Interview and Other Conversations* (Brooklyn, NY: Melville House, 2014), 43.

3. Ibid., 43–44.

4. Matt Buedel, "Forever Changed: Families of Two Slain Peorians Mourn amid Frustrations of Unsolved Case," *Journal Star* (Peoria, IL), January 20, 2014.

5. Richard Pryor with Todd Gold, *Pryor Convictions and Other Life Sentences* (New York: Pantheon Books, 1995), 247.

INDEX

blackness (cont.)
  social life of, 10–16, 32–36, 64–72,
    128–32, 139, 149*n*45; subjectivity
    and, 17–20, 82–86, 149*n*45, 150*n*49;
    value and, 8–9, 125–32; violence
    against, 113–14, 127–29, 138–39,
    163*n*1, 164*n*6. *See also* race; reality
    TV; representation; sexuality; women
Blackness and Value (Barrett), 129–30
Black Skins, White Masks (Fanon),
  149*n*45
black social life, 9–22, 32, 72, 98, 111, 116,
  125–26, 138, 149*n*45
bla(n)ckness (term), 22, 97–108
Blige, Mary J., 65, 73, 75, 157*n*29
Bomar, Vicki, 165*n*16
Brand, Myles, 115
Bright, Larry Dean, 114, 119, 122–23,
  163*n*1, 164*n*13
Brooks, Daphne, 22, 73
Brown, Frederickia, 163*n*1
Brown v. Board of Education, 13–14
Bynum, Juanita, 22, 54–63, 65, 155*n*16

Cacho, Lisa Marie, 118
capacity, 70, 90, 98, 102, 119–12
capitalism, 9, 18, 108–10, 112. *See also*
  citizenship; value(s)
Caterpillar, 2, 105–6, 162*n*43
Chicago, 1–3, 15, 131, 136–37, 139
Christian, Barbara, 98
churchgirlism, 43, 54–55, 136
citizenship, 15–16, 82–83, 127
Clark, Kenneth and Mamie, 13–14, 148*n*26
class, 7–12, 65, 108–10, 127, 139
Clifton, Lucille, 9
Clinton, Bill, 24, 98
COGIC (Church of God in Christ), 41,
  50. *See also* black church;
  Pentecostalism
Cohen, Cathy, 150*n*46

Cole, Keyshia, 65, 75–86, 157*n*29
College-Bound Assistance for
  Excellence, 89–90
College Hill (TV show), 25
Collins, Patricia Hill, 7, 18, 24, 68
Combahee River Collective, 7, 164*n*6
Cosby, Bill, 11
Crawley, Ashon, 62–63
craziness, 30–32, 38
Crenshaw, Kimberlé, 22

Davis, Erma, 89–90
death: black women's vulnerability and,
  113–16, 118–25; social, 11, 14–16, 18–19,
  111. *See also* serial murder
Denise (*Journal Star* subject), 90–91,
  92–94, 111
disavowal, 22–23, 29–30, 39, 49, 67, 95,
  115–18, 133, 149*n*45
Django Unchained (film), 8
domestic abuse, 55, 80–81, 84–86, 133
Dove, Rita, 6
drug addiction, 22, 76–86, 128–29
Drylongso (Gwaltney), 1, 127–28

Ellison, Ralph, 6, 9–10, 16
epidermalization, 95, 160*n*19
Erving, Brenda, 118–25, 128, 133–34
Erving, Carmea, 118–25, 131, 133, 165*n*18
Erving, Tyrhonda, 120–25, 131, 133, 165*n*18

Fabolous, 67
family structures, 105–12, 131–32
Fanon, Frantz, 95, 149*n*45
Fantasia, 65
feminism, 1–9, 15, 17–19, 22, 72–75.
  See also blackness; Combahee River
  Collective; sexuality; women; *specific
  scholars and writers*
Ferguson, Roderick A., 154*n*8
Fire Next Time, The (Baldwin), 40, 44

marriage, 54–61, 99–108. *See also*
    motherhood; sexuality; teenage
    pregnancy
McCarthy, Anna, 82–83
McCormick, Richard, 115
McCoy, Mike, 165*n*16
McMillan, Terry, 65, 155*n*1
McWhorter, John, 11
Melville, Herman, 125
Mercer, Kobena, 13
methodology, 20–22
misrecognition, 118
Morgan, Joan, 68
Morrison, Toni, 15, 22, 32–36, 125–29
Moten, Fred, 31, 128, 149*n*45, 153*n*19
motherhood, 59*n*12, 75–94, 98–112,
    159*n*4
Musson, Jayson, 30–31

nappy-headed ho(s), 114–18
National School-Age Mother and Child
    Health Act, 98
Native Son (Wright), 16, 117–18
Neal, Linda, 119, 122
neoliberalism, 82–84, 132
Nina (bachelorette party guest), 70–72, *71*
No More Sheets (Bynum), 55
"No More Sheets" (Bynum), 22, 54–62

Ouellette, Laurie, 82

pathology discourses, 11–14, 83–84,
    87–94, 98–108, 130–31
Patterson, Orlando, 11
Payne, Sabrina, 119
Pentecostalism, 40–42, 47–54, 154*n*14.
    See also black church
Peoria: as author's hometown, 2, 21–22,
    133, 138; bachelorette parties in, 64–72;
    blackness in, 15, 132–34; churches of,
    40–41; economic downturn in,

162*nn*43–44; *Journal Star* of, 22, 90,
    91–94, 97, 99–100, 104–5, 111; Richard
    Pryor and, 2, 132–34; serial murders
    in, 113–14, 118–25, 127; unwed mothers
    panic in, 87–95, 104–8
Personal Responsibility and Work
    Opportunity Act, 14
Petry, Ann, 130
Pollard, Tiffany, 25
Poussaint, Alvin, 11
poverty, 101–3, 107–8
pregnancy, 43–44, 77, 81, 87–94, 98–108,
    111, 138, 159*n*4, 159*n*12, 161*n*29
presence (affirmative), 24–32, 35–36,
    62–63, 94–98, 119–20, 125–27
Prison Notebooks (Gramsci), 18
prostitution, 75, 77, 85–86, 108–9, 113–14,
    116, 123–24, 128–32
proximity (to anger), 23–24, 26–28, 39
Pryor, Richard, 2, 132–34, 139
Pugh, Neffeteria "Neffe," 76–86

race: antagonism and, 22, 30, 85–86,
    133–34; citizenship and, 15–16, 82–83,
    127; class and, 11–12, 65, 83–84,
    109–10, 127, 139; color-blindness
    and, 14; neoliberalism and, 83–84;
    pathology discourses and, 11–16,
    83–94, 98–108, 130–31; Peoria's
    neighborhoods and, 135–39; police
    procedures and, 122–25, 127, 165*n*16;
    stereotype discourses and, 15–19,
    26–32, 53–54, 61, 67–69, 90, 102, 111,
    118, 157*n*30; surrogation and, 73–86;
    welfare recipients and, 13–14, 90–91,
    99, 104, 159*n*12. *See also* blackness;
    whiteness
Random 1 (TV show), 82–83
Rankine, Claudia, 30–31
R&B singers, 22, 64–86. *See also specific*
    artists

taxpayer rights, 14, 90–91, 99, 104, 159n12
Taylor, Mark, 94–95
teenage pregnancy, 87–94, 98–108, 159n4, 161n29
terror, 9, 14, 22, 117, 125, 128, 131, 138. *See also* blackness; whiteness
Thomas, Shaconda, 119
Tonéx, 22, 46–54, 63
tragic mulatto, 17
Trapp, Shirley Ann, 119
trauma, 47–48, 68, 78–83, 85–86, 165n16. *See also* sexuality; violence
Turner, Bernice Lee, 3–7, 9, 23, 138–39, 147n3
Turner, Patricia, 18

unthought, the, 18–19, 95–98, 110
"Unwed Parents" (*Journal Star* series), 90, 91–94, 96, 99–100, 103–5, 111

value(s): blackness and, 8–9, 125–32; bourgeois, 9–11; Marxian analysis and, 18, 108–12, 131; reproductive labor and, 108–12, 154n8; violence and, 133–34. *See also* Barrett, Lindon; capitalism; pathology discourses; respectability discourses
violence: bla(n)ckness and, 97–98, 128–30, 138–39, 163n1, 164n6; social death and, 11, 14–15; as stereotype, 17; value and, 133–34

Wade, Ernestine, 26
Wallace, Michele, 18
Walls, Tamara, 113, 119
Washington, Kerry, 8–9
Way It Is, The (Cole), 75
Weems, Renita, 55
welfare, 14, 61, 69, 82, 90–91, 98–99, 101–2, 104–6, 159n12
welfare queen, 14, 61, 90, 102, 111

Wellman, David, 11–12
White, Deborah Gray, 18
White, Karyn, 65–72
whiteness: black grotesque and, 94–98; black presence and, 24–32, 35–36, 62–63, 94–98, 119–20, 125–27; black social life's denigration and, 11–16; Morrison on, 125–26; unwed mothers and, 100–101. *See also* blackness; race
Wilderson, Frank, 14, 18–19, 30–31, 110, 138
Williams, Barbara, 119
Williams, Delores, 73
Williams, Juan, 11
Williams, Serena, 30–32
Williamson, Terrion L.: anger and, 37–40; bachelorette party experiences of, 64–72; churchgirlism and, 40–46, 54–55; graduate education of, 113–14; grandmother of, 1–7, 9–10, 23, 138–39, 147n3; Peoria's unwed mother panic and, 87–90
Winfrey, Oprah, 8–9
women: anger and, 23–36, 38–40; black church and, 7, 40–46, 48–55, 57–64; "craziness" and, 30–32, 34–36, 38; the grotesque and, 94–98; "in the life" trope and, 22, 85–86, 118–19, 123–25, 133–34; moral disciplining of, 26–29, 34–36, 40–46, 87–98; motherhood and, 59n12, 75–94, 98–112, 159n4; R&B singers and, 65–86; reproductive value of, 108–12; social intimacy and, 22, 32–36, 42–43, 64–75, 78–86, 108–12, 128–32, 139; stereotyping and, 15, 17–19, 61, 67–68; surrogation and, 73–86. *See also* blackness; feminism; sexuality; value(s); violence
"The World and the Jug" (Ellison), 16
World Foot Locker, 136–37, 167n1
Wright, Richard, 16, 117–18

J. Hillis Miller, *Communities in Fiction*.

Remo Bodei, *The Life of Things, the Love of Things*. Translated by Murtha Baca.

Gabriela Basterra, *The Subject of Freedom: Kant, Levinas*.

Roberto Esposito, *Categories of the Impolitical*. Translated by Connal Parsley.

Roberto Esposito, *Two: The Machine of Political Theology and the Place of Thought*. Translated by Zakiya Hanafi.

Akiba Lerner, *Redemptive Hope: From the Age of Enlightenment to the Age of Obama*.

Adriana Cavarero and Angelo Scola, *Thou Shalt Not Kill: A Political and Theological Dialogue*. Translated by Margaret Adams Groesbeck and Adam Sitze.

Massimo Cacciari, *Europe and Empire: On the Political Forms of Globalization*. Edited by Alessandro Carrera. Translated by Massimo Verdicchio.

Emanuele Coccia, *Sensible Life: A Micro-ontology of the Image*. Translated by Scott Stuart. Introduction by Kevin Attell.

Timothy C. Campbell, *The Techne of Giving: Cinema and the Generous Forms of Life*.

Étienne Balibar, *Citizen Subject: Foundations for Philosophical Anthropology*. Translated by Steven Miller. Foreword by Emily Apter.

Ashon T. Crawley, *Blackpentecostal Breath: The Aesthetics of Possibility*.

Terrion L. Williamson, *Scandalize My Name: Black Feminist Practice and the Making of Black Social Life*.

Jean-Luc Nancy, *The Disavowed Community*. Translated by Philip Armstrong.